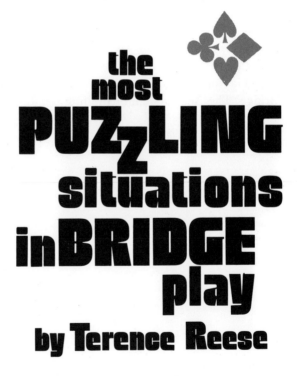

the most PUZZLING situations in BRIDGE play

by Terence Reese

STERLING PUBLISHING CO., INC.   NEW YORK

Books by Terence Reese

Terence Reese has written about 45 books on bridge, poker, canasta and backgammon. These are some of his most important books on bridge:

Begin Bridge with Reese*
Reese on Play
The Expert Game (in America, "Master Play")
Play Bridge with Reese*
Develop Your Bidding Judgment*
Play These Hands with Me
The Bridge Player's Dictionary*
The Blue Club
Precision Bidding and Precision Play*
Bridge at the Top
    with Albert Dormer:
The Complete Book of Bridge
The Play of the Cards
Bridge: The Acol System of Bidding

*Published by Sterling

Contents

Foreword

Most books containing problems are not arranged in any systematic way. The reader may enjoy the mental stimulus, as he may enjoy doing a crossword, but whether he will improve his game to any extent with such books is doubtful.

I have aimed here at something different. I have thought of eight puzzling situations, or themes, that constantly recur but are not the usual textbook material. These themes are introduced with a few pages of explanation, and a group of problems follows. The idea is to fix the type of play in the reader's mind.

A comparison with golf may help to illustrate the difference between the average quiz book and this one. You may spend three or four hours on a round of golf, playing a variety of shots, but in the process you will improve your game only to a very, very small degree. But if you devote the same amount of time to particular shots, such as bunker shots or chip shots from a given distance, you will really get somewhere.

Let it be said that some of the problems are far from easy: even a player of international class might fail to find the best answer. Do not assume, therefore, if you don't get the answer first time, that you are out of your depth and learning nothing. Take each section slowly and return to it after a few months of play. You will be surprised, then, to find how much easier it all seems.

I have been most fortunate to have the assistance of David Greenwood, who read the proofs and made many perceptive comments. In return, I have even altered some bidding sequences that pained him.

TERENCE REESE

1. Averting a Ruff

"It was only the ruff that beat us." How many times have those sad words been the epitaph on a lost contract!

Let us begin with the simplest way of all to prevent a ruff: simply draw trumps.

$$
\begin{array}{l}
\spadesuit \text{J 8 5} \\
\heartsuit \text{9 7 6 2} \\
\diamondsuit \text{K Q 8} \\
\clubsuit \text{Q 7 3}
\end{array}
$$

$\heartsuit$ Q led

$$
\begin{array}{l}
\spadesuit \text{K Q 10 9 6 2} \\
\heartsuit \text{A 8} \\
\diamondsuit \text{A 4} \\
\clubsuit \text{K 10 6}
\end{array}
$$

South is in four spades, and West leads the queen of hearts. As a problem in play it should not be difficult, yet at the table how many players would win with the ace of hearts and attempt to discard a losing heart on the third round of diamonds! Unlucky! Diamonds are 6–2 and West ruffs. True, after West ruffs and plays ace and another spade the declarer still has chances, but in the end he will probably have to finesse the 10 of clubs for his contract.

The fault here lies simply in not counting winning tricks. Declarer has on top five spades, three diamonds, one heart, and one club. Nothing can go wrong if he draws trumps, but by trying for the discard on the third round of diamonds he puts one of his certain tricks at risk. In a pairs contest this would be a fair gamble because of the chance of making an overtrick, but at any other form of scoring it would be madness.

A second method to avert a ruff: Protect your master cards. Suppose you have this type of holding in a side suit:

$$\diamondsuit \text{A 7 5}$$

$$\diamondsuit \text{K 6 4 2}$$

You are playing in a suit contract, the ace of trumps is out against you, and West leads the 8 of this side suit. Well, if there is a singleton in either hand, East is likely to hold it, because West, from a holding headed by Q J 10 8 or J 10 9 8, would not have led the 8. So the safety play to protect one of the high cards from being ruffed is to win the first trick with the king. If the 8 was a singleton West may obtain a ruff later, but he will be ruffing a loser.

Suppose, next, that the opening lead was not the 8 but the queen. Now it is much more likely that West has led from five cards headed by the queen than from a singleton queen. The correct play, therefore, to guard against a singleton in the East hand, is the ace from dummy at trick one.

There are many forms of avoidance play where the object is to protect master cards from an untimely ruff. Suppose you are developing a side suit such as:

♣ 7 5 3

♣ A K 9 6 2

It might be a mistake to lead out ace and king because if East turns up with a singleton he will ruff one of these high cards. It is better technique to cash the ace and cross to dummy for the next lead. If East ruffs, he will be ruffing a loser.

Here the same principle appears in more exaggerated form:

```
                 ♠ A 10 8
                 ♡ 10 7 5 4
                 ◇ A 9 6 3
                 ♣ 6 2
 ♠ 6 5 2            ┌──────────┐      ♠ 7 4
 ♡ J 8 6 2         │    N     │      ♡ Q 9 3
 ◇ Q J 10 4 2      │ W     E  │      ◇ K 7 5
 ♣ 4               │    S     │      ♣ Q J 10 8 5
                   └──────────┘
                 ♠ K Q J 9 3
                 ♡ A K
 ◇ Q led         ◇ 8
                 ♣ A K 9 7 3
```

South is in six spades and West leads the queen of diamonds

to dummy's ace. When the ace of clubs wins the second trick, declarer should follow, not with the king of clubs, but a low club. You see why it would be wrong to continue with the king? West would ruff and play a trump, leaving declarer with three losing clubs and only two trumps in dummy.

There are many clever ways of cutting the opponents' communications so that they cannot obtain a ruff. This is known as the Scissors Coup:

```
                    ♠ 10 8 5 2
                    ♡ K 5 4
                    ◇ A 10 2
                    ♣ J 9 5
  ♠ A Q 6 4          ┌─────────┐          ♠ K J 9 7
  ♡ 3                │    N    │          ♡ J 9 8 6 2
  ◇ Q 9 8 6 3        │ W     E │          ◇ 7 5 4
  ♣ A 6 2            │    S    │          ♣ 4
                     └─────────┘
  ♡ 3 led           ♠ 3
                    ♡ A Q 10 7
                    ◇ K J
                    ♣ K Q 10 8 7 3
```

South plays in five clubs after West has opened one diamond and East has responded one heart. West leads the 3 of hearts, which is very likely to be a singleton. If South plays in normal fashion, attacking trumps, West will underlead his A Q of spades and obtain a ruff. Declarer can prevent this by cutting the opponents' communications. He plays king of diamonds, jack of diamonds to the ace, and 10 of diamonds, discarding a spade. The spade loser has been exchanged for a diamond loser, and now West cannot give his partner the lead.

A fourth way of averting a ruff is to "Remove the offending object." Suppose that declarer has a side suit of this nature:

◇ K Q 6 4

◇ A 5

He plays ace, king, queen, discarding on the third round. If he now attacks trumps he may be exposed to a fourth round of the same suit, perhaps leading to an opponent's trump promotion. Declarer may be able to prevent this by continuing with a fourth diamond himself, discarding another loser.

One other way to avert a ruff is to cash top cards in a suit before the ruff can materialize. This rather tricky theme is illustrated in two of the examples that follow.

Dealer, North   Neither side vulnerable

```
                    ♠ K 8 5
                    ♡ A Q J 9 4
                    ◇ 7 5
                    ♣ A Q 7
    ◇  10 led
                    ♠ J 10 7 6 4 2
                    ♡ K 5
                    ◇ K 6
                    ♣ K 8 2
```

South	West	North	East
—	—	1 ♡	2 ◇
2 ♠	pass	4 ♠ (1)	pass
pass	pass		

Final contract—Four Spades

(1) This may seem a slight overbid, but the sequence is one where a slight overbid is often well-advised. South's response at the two level *might* have embarrassed North; since North is worth three-and-a-half spades he does well to take the strain off partner by bidding the game.

The early play

West leads the 10 of diamonds, East plays the jack and South wins with the king. How should South plan the play?

First look

South can afford to lose two spades and a diamond, so prospects seem good. Is there, however, a portent in the sky?

Problem No. 1

It seems natural to run the 10 of spades at trick two. This gives the defenders their chance, as you will see from the full diagram:

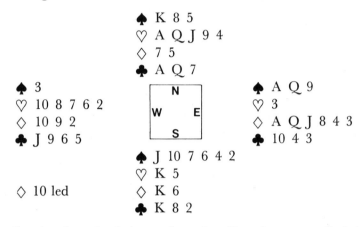

                ♠ K 8 5
                ♡ A Q J 9 4
                ◇ 7 5
                ♣ A Q 7

♠ 3   ♠ A Q 9
♡ 10 8 7 6 2   ♡ 3
◇ 10 9 2   ◇ A Q J 8 4 3
♣ J 9 6 5   ♣ 10 4 3

                ♠ J 10 7 6 4 2
                ♡ K 5
◇ 10 led   ◇ K 6
                ♣ K 8 2

South plays in four spades after East has overcalled in diamonds. West's lead of the 10 of diamonds is covered by East's jack, and South's king wins. If South now finesses the 10 of spades at trick two, East will win and lead his singleton heart. However the play goes from this point, East will play his partner for the 9 of diamonds and put him in for a heart return. The ruff will beat the contract.

Good work by East, but South should not have missed the significance of East's play of the jack of diamonds on the opening lead. East has played the jack to force the king and create a situation that will allow him to give his partner the lead on the next round of the suit. The solution: South must break the link by returning a diamond himself at trick two. This timely play destroys the defensive link.

Dealer, North Both sides vulnerable

$$
\begin{array}{l}
\spadesuit \ \text{K} \\
\heartsuit \ \text{Q 6 2} \\
\diamondsuit \ \text{A K 4 2} \\
\clubsuit \ \text{A Q 7 4 3}
\end{array}
$$

$\diamondsuit$ 10 led

$$
\begin{array}{l}
\spadesuit \ \text{Q J 5} \\
\heartsuit \ \text{J 10 9 8 5 3} \\
\diamondsuit \ \text{Q J 7} \\
\clubsuit \ \text{6}
\end{array}
$$

South	West	North	East
—	—	1 ♣	pass
1 ♡	pass	2 ◇	pass
2 ♡	pass	3 ♡ (1)	pass
4 ♡ (2)	pass	pass	pass

Final contract—Four Hearts

(1) Close to four hearts, perhaps, but North must bear in mind that partner was more or less obliged to say something over the reverse of two diamonds and may be quite weak.

(2) Borderline, but the hearts are respectable and the bidding suggests that partner may have a singleton spade.

The early play

West leads the 10 of diamonds, dummy plays the king and East the 5. How should South plan the play?

First look

The hands fit fairly well and there are only three top losers. However, the diamond lead contains a possible threat.

Problem No. 2

When this deal occurred in a pairs event the South players adopted different schemes to avert the threatened ruff in diamonds. The more naive thought that the best plan would be to lead trumps as soon as possible. This proved a failure, for the full hand was:

```
                    ♠ K
                    ♡ Q 6 2
                    ◇ A K 4 2
                    ♣ A Q 7 4 3
  ♠ 9 7 6 3 2          N          ♠ A 10 8 4
  ♡ A 7 4                         ♡ K
  ◇ 10 9          W     E         ◇ 8 6 5 3
  ♣ J 8 5             S           ♣ K 10 9 2

                    ♠ Q J 5
                    ♡ J 10 9 8 5 3
  ◇ 10 led          ◇ Q J 7
                    ♣ 6
```

Say that South, playing in four hearts, wins the diamond lead in dummy and plays a trump at trick two. East will win and lead another diamond. When West comes in with the ace of hearts he will give partner the lead in spades and a diamond ruff will be the fourth trick for the defenders.

Some players decided that a spade at trick two might interrupt the communications. East won and played a second diamond, but when declarer played trumps he came in with the king and gave partner the diamond ruff, as before.

Still more unfortunate was a declarer who tried a club finesse to dispose of his third diamond. This resulted in a two-trick defeat.

The best play seemed to be a blind spot for the majority. It was right to lead a spade at trick two. When East won and led a second diamond, all that was required—logical though none too obvious—was to win with the queen and discard two diamonds from dummy on the Q J of spades. Then the danger of a ruff disappeared.

Dealer, South   Neither side vulnerable

♠ 10 7 6 4 2
♡ 5 3
◇ A K
♣ J 7 4 3

◇ J led

♠ A K
♡ K J 10 9 8 7
◇ 8 4 2
♣ K 6

South	West	North	East
1 ♡	pass	1 ♠	pass
3 ♡ (1)	pass	4 ♡ (2)	pass
pass	pass		

Final contract—Four Hearts

(1) Some players would rebid only two hearts, but South has, after all, about seven playing tricks in his own hand.

(2) The doubleton A K of diamonds and the two low trumps suggest a raise of partner's suit rather than an attempt to play in 3NT.

The early play

West leads the jack of diamonds. Needing to ruff the third round of diamonds, declarer cashes the ace and king, then crosses to the ace of spades. How should he continue?

First look

South can afford to lose two hearts and one club, or one heart and two clubs. One problem is that he is short of entries to dummy, even if he assumes that the diamond ruff will stand up.

Problem No. 3

The trickiest problems are those that divert attention from the most difficult area. It is easy for South to think, "When in dummy I must lead a club, not a heart, as the heart would gain only against Q x in the East hand." True, but the main point, as we shall see, is that declarer must concentrate on protecting his winners.

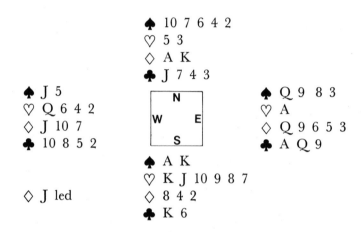

Playing in four hearts, South wins the diamond lead in dummy, cashes a second diamond, and crosses to the ace of spades. Suppose he now ruffs a diamond and leads a club from the dummy.

East, who has dropped the queen of diamonds on the third round, goes up with the ace of clubs and meanly produces a fourth diamond. South ruffs and West discards a spade. South leads the king of hearts (there may be a singleton queen out), East wins and gives his partner a ruff in spades. Mysteriously, the lay-down contract has been defeated.

Paradoxical as it may seem, the way to avert a spade ruff is to cash a second round at an early stage. The principle is the same as when a declarer cashes side winners before embarking on a crossruff: he prevents dangerous discards by extracting the card that might otherwise be discarded.

Dealer, South   Both sides vulnerable

♠ K 8 7 3
♡ A J 4
◇ 10 5
♣ Q 9 4 2

♠ J led

♠ A 5
♡ —
◇ A Q J 9 8 7 3
♣ K J 10 6

South	West	North	East
1◇	pass	1♠	pass
3◇	pass	3NT	pass
4♣	pass	4◇(1)	pass
5◇	pass	pass	pass

Final contract—Five Diamonds

(1) Partner's bidding suggests 6–4 or 7–4 distribution in the minor suits, and North is right to give preference to diamonds. Top-heavy hands almost always play best in the long suit.

The early play

West leads the jack of spades. How should South plan the play?

First look

One trick must be lost to the ace of clubs and possibly one to the king of diamonds. It looks as though only a ruff will beat the contract.

Problem No. 4

Aware of the danger of a club ruff, the declarer won the spade lead and played off ace and another diamond. This was right up to a point, but disaster struck from another quarter.

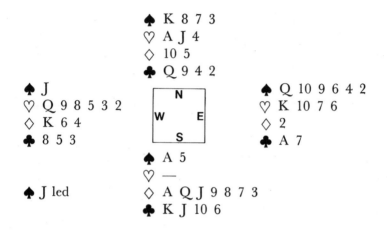

♠ K 8 7 3
♡ A J 4
◇ 10 5
♣ Q 9 4 2

♠ J
♡ Q 9 8 5 3 2
◇ K 6 4
♣ 8 5 3

♠ Q 10 9 6 4 2
♡ K 10 7 6
◇ 2
♣ A 7

♠ A 5
♡ —
♠ J led   ◇ A Q J 9 8 7 3
♣ K J 10 6

When West came in with the king of diamonds he put his partner in with the ace of clubs and ruffed the next spade, to defeat the contract.

Unlucky, but South had omitted a slight precaution. It would have cost nothing to win the first trick with the king of spades and discard the ace of spades on the ace of hearts, avoiding all danger of a spade ruff.

After taking the discard, it is a close question whether South should finesse in trumps or play off ace and another. To finesse will lose when West holds K x of diamonds and there is a singleton club on either side, also when West has a singleton king of diamonds and East has a singleton club. To play off ace and another will cost when East has K x x or K x x x in diamonds and a singleton club. My instinct would be to take the finesse.

Dealer, South   Both sides vulnerable

♠ J 7 5 3
♡ 10 7 6 4 3
♢ 5 4
♣ 9 5

♠ K led

♠ —
♡ J
♢ A K Q 10 7 6 2
♣ A K Q 3 2

South	West	North	East
2♢	pass	2NT	pass
3♣(1)	pass	3♡	pass
4♢	pass	5♢	pass
· pass(2)	pass		

Final contract—Five Diamonds

(1) With 6–4 or 7–4 distribution it is usually best to bid the suits in the order long-long-short, but with 6–5 or 7–5 long-short-long. This tells partner that the second suit is of five-card length.

(2) On the cautious side, but South is not entitled to place partner with the ace of hearts and does not regard the club suit as necessarily solid.

The early play

West leads the king of spades. South ruffs and lays down the ace of diamonds, on which East discards a spade. How should South continue?

First look

South may be glad that he bid the hand nervously. It looks now as though he must lose a heart, a trump and quite possibly a club.

Problem No. 5

In a team event South failed to gain a swing against opponents who had contracted for six diamonds.

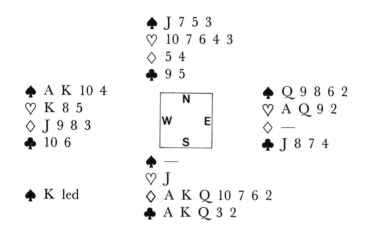

```
                    ♠ J 7 5 3
                    ♡ 10 7 6 4 3
                    ◇ 5 4
                    ♣ 9 5
♠ A K 10 4                              ♠ Q 9 8 6 2
♡ K 8 5                                 ♡ A Q 9 2
◇ J 9 8 3                               ◇ —
♣ 10 6                                  ♣ J 8 7 4
                    ♠ —
                    ♡ J
♠ K led             ◇ A K Q 10 7 6 2
                    ♣ A K Q 3 2
```

Playing in five diamonds, South ruffed the spade lead and cashed the ace of diamonds, discovering that he had a trump loser. He then turned to the clubs, playing ace, king and a low one. As might have been expected, West ruffed in front of dummy with the 8 of diamonds and led the 8 of hearts to his partner's ace. East led a fourth club and West made another trump, to defeat the contract.

South missed a rather tricky example of the Scissors Coup. He should have cut the communications between the defending hands by leading the jack of hearts after one round of diamonds. If West takes the trick he cannot lead a second round of trumps without giving up his trump trick. The difference is that when West ruffs the third round of clubs he cannot put his partner in with a heart to play a fourth club.

Dealer, North   Both sides vulnerable

<pre>
                    ♠ A K 10 6 2
                    ♡ A K Q
                    ◇ K 6 4
                    ♣ Q 9
    ◇ Q led

                    ♠ 5 4
                    ♡ 10 9 8 7 6 4 2
                    ◇ A 9 7 3
                    ♣ —
</pre>

South	*West*	*North*	*East*
—	—	1♠	4♣
4♡	pass	4NT	pass
5◇(1)	pass	6♡(2)	pass
pass	pass		

Final contract—Six Hearts

(1) In some versions of the Blackwood convention a jump to six clubs at this point would indicate an ace and a void. Such a bid would be unwise here, as South's trumps are moderate.

(2) There might theoretically be two losing clubs in each hand, but North takes the view that with two club losers and trumps headed by the jack at best, South, having already bid four hearts, would have declined to show his ace over 4NT. In any case, North knows that the slam will be missed unless he bids it himself.

The early play

West leads the queen of diamonds. South plays low from dummy, partly because he does not want to risk the possibility of the king being ruffed, and partly because he may need entries to dummy to set up a long spade. East follows to the diamond but discards a club on the first round of trumps. How should South continue?

First look

There are eleven top winners and would have been twelve if trumps had broken 2–1. As it is, the declarer needs to develop an extra trick either in spades or diamonds.

Problem No. 6

No doubt West has led from a strong sequence in diamonds, and the best chance is to develop a long card in spades. As East is marked by the bidding with long clubs, it seems fairly safe to play ace, king and another spade. If the suit is divided 4–2, South will be able to draw trumps, ruff another spade, and enter dummy with the king of diamonds to make a trick with the fifth spade.

This plan goes awry because the distribution is:

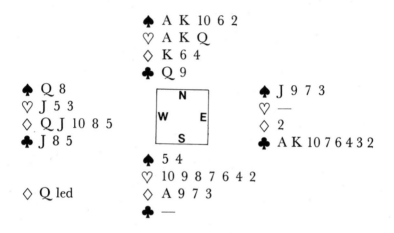

♠ A K 10 6 2
♡ A K Q
♢ K 6 4
♣ Q 9

♠ Q 8
♡ J 5 3
♢ Q J 10 8 5
♣ J 8 5

♠ J 9 7 3
♡ —
♢ 2
♣ A K 10 7 6 4 3 2

♠ 5 4
♡ 10 9 8 7 6 4 2
♢ A 9 7 3
♣ —

◇ Q led

Playing in six hearts, South wins the diamond lead in his own hand, plays a round of trumps, then ace, king and another spade. But alas! West, after all, is short of spades and overruffs the 10 of hearts with the jack. South can set up a long spade, but must still lose a diamond.

"It wouldn't have helped to draw trumps," the declarer remarks, "because then I am short of an entry to enjoy the fifth spade."

True, but South can improve his chances by leading the queen of clubs after one round of trumps and discarding a spade. This cunning move allows him to ruff the second round of spades in safety. He can then draw trumps, ruff another spade and cross to the king of diamonds to make the K 10 of spades.

Dealer, West   E–W vulnerable

```
              ♠ 8 7 3
              ♡ A K J 7 4
              ◇ A Q 10
              ♣ Q 10

♣ K led

              ♠ A Q J 6 2
              ♡ 10 5
              ◇ J 8 4
              ♣ 8 5 2
```

South	West	North	East
—	1NT	dble	pass
pass	2♣	pass	pass
2♠	pass	3♠(1)	pass
4♠	pass	pass	pass

Final contract—Four Spades

(1) As North has already doubled a strong notrump opening by West, this raise is borderline. However, he can be sure that his partner holds five spades and the fact that he passed the double of 1NT suggests that he has some values.

The early play

West begins with king, ace and jack of clubs, East following suit with the 4, 7 and 9. After ruffing the third round in dummy, how should South plan the play?

First look

South can be confident of the diamond finesse being right, so he needs only to avoid losing two tricks in spades.

Problem No. 7

The declarer's first thought may be that it would be dangerous to finesse the queen of spades, because West, holding K 10 x or K 9 x, might play a fourth club, leading to a trump promotion. In any case, the spade finesse is sure to lose, so why not lead out ace and queen, to prevent East from ruffing with a doubleton in trumps? The answer is that this may not be enough.

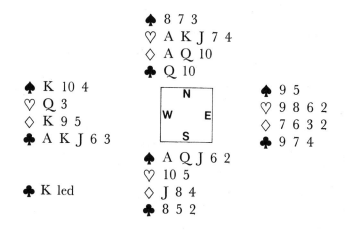

```
                  ♠ 8 7 3
                  ♡ A K J 7 4
                  ◇ A Q 10
                  ♣ Q 10
♠ K 10 4                        ♠ 9 5
♡ Q 3              N            ♡ 9 8 6 2
◇ K 9 5         W     E         ◇ 7 6 3 2
♣ A K J 6 3        S            ♣ 9 7 4
                  ♠ A Q J 6 2
♣ K led           ♡ 10 5
                  ◇ J 8 4
                  ♣ 8 5 2
```

South plays in four spades after West has opened 1NT and after being doubled has rescued himself into two clubs.

The defenders begin with three rounds of clubs, South ruffing in dummy. To prevent a trump promotion arising from the ruff of a fourth round of clubs, South plays ace and queen of spades. West wins and exits with a heart. Suddenly, the contract cannot be made, because declarer cannot come off the table without losing to the king of diamonds or allowing West to overruff the third round of hearts.

This unseemly end can be prevented by playing off ace and king of hearts before playing trumps. South cannot then be planted in the dummy, with no safe exit. The contract would be equally safe if West held a third heart.

Dealer, North   Neither side vulnerable

```
                        ♠ 10 6 5 2
                        ♡ A Q J 4
                        ◇ 4
                        ♣ J 7 6 3
◇ 10 led
                        ♠ Q 9 8 4 3
                        ♡ 10 7
                        ◇ A K J 2
                        ♣ K 9
```

South	West	North	East
—	—	pass	pass
1♠	dble	2NT(1)	pass
4♠(2)	pass	pass	pass

Final contract—Four Spades

(1) After West's take-out double this bid conventionally shows the values for a sound raise to three spades.

(2) South must bid game now, because three spades would be a sign-off.

The early play

West leads the 10 of diamonds, East plays the queen and South wins. How should South plan the play?

First look

There is duplication in diamonds and South has several possible losers. A successful finesse in hearts will enable him to discard one club, but this will not necessarily be the end of the matter.

Problem No. 8

South began on the right lines but was struck down by a blow that he had not foreseen.

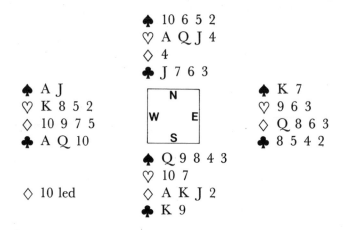

♠ 10 6 5 2
♡ A Q J 4
◇ 4
♣ J 7 6 3

♠ A J
♡ K 8 5 2
◇ 10 9 7 5
♣ A Q 10

♠ K 7
♡ 9 6 3
◇ Q 8 6 3
♣ 8 5 4 2

♠ Q 9 8 4 3
♡ 10 7
◇ A K J 2
♣ K 9

◇ 10 led

South played in four spades after West had made a take-out double of one spade. South won the diamond lead and correctly led the 10 of hearts at trick two. This finesse had to be taken sooner or later and South had hopes of obtaining a club discard.

West played low on the heart lead, so South repeated the finesse and discarded a club on the ace of hearts. Hoping now to lose just two trumps and a club, he led a spade from dummy, finessing the 8. West won with the jack, cashed the ace of clubs and led a fourth heart. East ruffed with the king of spades, so the defenders made three tricks in trumps and the ace of clubs.

It is important in this type of situation to play loser-on-loser, disposing of the card that may allow the opponents to make their high trumps separately. South must play a fourth round of hearts himself, discarding the king of clubs. The defenders make this trick, and thereafter only two trump tricks.

2. Which Suit First?

Which suit should you attack first? In notrump contracts there are a few general rules, such as (a) play on the suit that will provide you with enough tricks for the contract, or (b) a suit in which you have top losers that must be forced out. But these are only general rules and there are many exceptions.

```
                    ♠ K 8 4
                    ♡ Q J 5
                    ◇ K J 3
                    ♣ A 10 7 4
♡ 4 led
                    ♠ A 10
                    ♡ A 7 2
                    ◇ Q 5 4
                    ♣ Q J 9 8 3
```

You are in 3NT and West leads the 4 of hearts. Dummy's queen holds the trick, East dropping the 6.

Now the lazy play is to enter hand with the ace of spades and finesse the queen of clubs. A successful finesse will give you enough tricks and in any case you will need club tricks for your contract. But if the finesse loses and East returns a heart you will be defeated whenever West began with ♡K x x x x and ace of diamonds. To ensure your ninth trick you must set up a winner in diamonds first. If the opponents do not take their diamond trick you shift at once to clubs. To play a second diamond would be a mistake if East held ◇A 10 x x x and king of clubs and you only need one diamond trick anyway.

This is another deal where it would be a mistake to play on the long suit first:

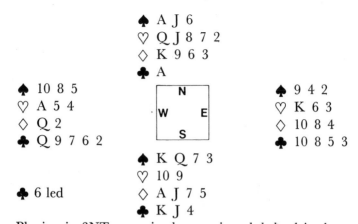

♠ A J 6
♡ Q J 8 7 2
◇ K 9 6 3
♣ A

♠ 10 8 5
♡ A 5 4
◇ Q 2
♣ Q 9 7 6 2

N W E S

♠ 9 4 2
♡ K 6 3
◇ 10 8 4
♣ 10 8 5 3

♠ K Q 7 3
♡ 10 9
◇ A J 7 5
♣ K J 4

♣ 6 led

Playing in 3NT you win the opening club lead in dummy. If you lead a heart at trick two, any experienced player in the East position will go up with the king to protect his partner's entries and will lead a second club. Now you will lose the contract unless you are sufficiently inspired to drop the doubleton queen of diamonds. There is a completely safe line: lead a diamond to the ace at trick two, intending, if necessary, to finesse the 9 on the next round. This will ensure three diamond tricks, enough for game.

Very often, the play in one suit will tell you how to play another suit.

♠ —
♡ K 8 5 3 2
◇ A Q 6 2
♣ K J 5 4

♠ K led

♠ A 7 4
♡ A Q 9 6
◇ 7 5 4
♣ A 8 3

Playing in six hearts, you win the spade lead in hand, play a heart to the king and draw two more rounds. The next play should be a finesse of ◇ Q. If this loses, you must play to make four tricks in clubs, but if it wins you can make the safety play in clubs—king, ace, and low to the jack. This gains when East has a doubleton queen.

Dealer, South   Neither side vulnerable

♠ K 4 3
♡ A K J 10 6 5
◇ K 4
♣ K 6

◇ 9 led

♠ A J 10 9 8
♡ 9 3
◇ A Q J
♣ A Q 2

South	West	North	East
1♠	pass	2♡(1)	pass
3NT	pass	4♣(2)	pass
4♠	pass	4NT	pass
5♠	pass	7NT(3)	pass
pass	pass		

Final contract—7NT

(1) Obviously North has the values for a forcing response, but when there are various features the responder may wish to express (the good hearts, the spade support, the all-round strength) it is often better to start with a simple reply.

(2) At this point North is fishing for heart support, which will encourage him to move towards a grand slam.

(3) Having discovered that his partner holds three aces, North judges that if either major suit can be run without loss there must be an excellent chance for thirteen tricks.

The early play

West leads the 9 of diamonds, East plays the 2, and South wins in hand with the queen. How should South plan the play?

First look

As North had surmised in the bidding, South needs only to run one of the major suits to make the grand slam. His problem is how to combine the chances to the best effect.

Problem No. 9

On some hands of this type it would be good play to take three rounds of the unimportant suits, diamonds and clubs in this case, because some clue to the distribution might turn up. This would not be a good idea here, because entries in the minor suits might be needed to enable the declarer to play the major suits to the best advantage.

As there are eight cards in each major suit, the chance of dropping the queen in two rounds is the same in each suit. Nevertheless, there is a sound reason for playing on hearts first. The distinction appears when the hand is as follows:

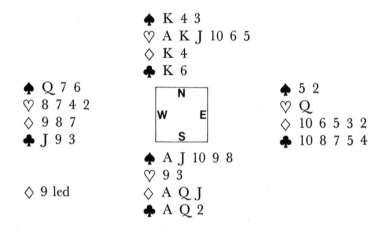

♠ K 4 3
♡ A K J 10 6 5
♢ K 4
♣ K 6

♠ Q 7 6
♡ 8 7 4 2
♢ 9 8 7
♣ J 9 3

♠ 5 2
♡ Q
♢ 10 6 5 3 2
♣ 10 8 7 5 4

♢ 9 led

♠ A J 10 9 8
♡ 9 3
♢ A Q J
♣ A Q 2

South is in 7NT and West leads a diamond. If the ace and king of hearts are played off and the queen does not fall, declarer can play the spades to the best advantage, leading the king and then finessing, winning against Q x x x (or fewer) in the East hand. But if the ace and king of spades are played off without any result, the best play in hearts is to run the 9 on the first round, gaining against Q x x x in the West hand, but losing to a singleton queen. Which would be very expensive as the cards lie!

To state the point again: if South plays on hearts first he can still play the spades in the best possible way, but if he plays on spades first he may lose later to a singleton queen of hearts. Better, therefore, to begin by playing off the top hearts.

Dealer, North   Neither side vulnerable

                        ♠ A Q 10 6 4 2
                        ♡ A K J 5
                        ◇ 6
                        ♣ K 5

◇ K led

                        ♠ K 7
                        ♡ 8 7 3
                        ◇ A J 10 5
                        ♣ A J 6 2

South	West	North	East
—	—	1♠	pass
2♣	pass	2♡(1)	pass
3NT	pass	4NT(2)	pass
6NT(3)	pass	pass	pass

Final contract—6NT

(1) The change of suit after a response at the two level is generally played as forcing, so there is no need to jump.

(2) North can see slam possibilities and four clubs is an alternative worth considering. As no suit has been agreed, 4NT is natural, not conventional.

(3) South has not much in hand, but the diamond holding is strong and he has a fit for his partner's first suit.

The early play

West leads the king of diamonds and East plays the 3. How should South plan the play?

First look

If the spades are breaking, South has eleven tricks on top and several chances for a twelfth. He must decide whether to win the first trick and what to play next.

Problem No. 10

When this hand occurred at rubber bridge, the declarer counted six spades, two hearts, two clubs and, after the lead, two diamonds. Realizing that if he ran the spades he would lack the entries to establish his second trick in diamonds, he won the first trick with the ace of diamonds and at once returned the jack. At this point he had to find a discard from the dummy.

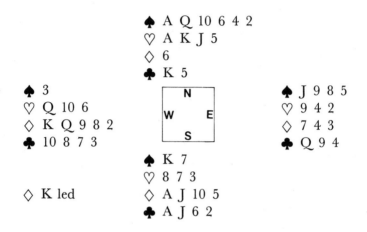

♠ A Q 10 6 4 2
♡ A K J 5
♢ 6
♣ K 5

♠ 3
♡ Q 10 6
♢ K Q 9 8 2
♣ 10 8 7 3

♠ J 9 8 5
♡ 9 4 2
♢ 7 4 3
♣ Q 9 4

♢ K led

♠ K 7
♡ 8 7 3
♢ A J 10 5
♣ A J 6 2

As he was not expecting to use dummy's hearts, South discarded the 5 from dummy. West exited with the nine of diamonds and South now discarded the jack of hearts. Unfortunately, when he played king and another spade, the suit did not break 3–2. The best he could do was give up a spade to East and go one down, as East had no more diamonds.

South observed with some annoyance that as the hearts and clubs lay, he could have made sufficient tricks without using the long spades. The correct play after winning the first trick with the ace of diamonds was to test the spades by playing low to the ace and back to the king. When he finds that the spades do not break, South plays the jack of diamonds, discarding a spade from dummy. With both finesses right and the hearts 3–3, South can arrive at twelve tricks by straightforward play.

Dealer, South   Neither side vulnerable

```
              ♠ K 3 2
              ♡ A 5 3
              ◇ A Q
              ♣ K Q 6 4 3
♠ Q led
              ♠ A 8 7 6 5 4
              ♡ K J 4 2
              ◇ J
              ♣ A 2
```

South	West	North	East
1♠	pass	2♣(1)	pass
2♠	pass	3◇	pass
3NT(2)	pass	5♠	pass
6♠	pass	pass	pass

Final contract—Six Spades

(1) It seems to be the fashion nowadays to force only with a powerful suit or strong support for partner's suit. I don't think the failure to force makes hands of this type any easier to manage, but the present slam is simple by any method.

(2) Three hearts at this point would be "fourth suit," denying rather than asserting a good guard in hearts.

The early play

West leads the queen of spades. South wins in dummy and leads a second spade, on which East discards a high diamond. South switches to ace and another club, West discarding a diamond on the second round. How should South continue?

First look

After the disappointment of finding trumps 3–1 and clubs 5–1, South is one trick short. It looks as though he will need a successful finesse in one of the red suits.

Problem No. 11

South can improve on the chance of a simple finesse by playing off ace and king of hearts. If the queen does not fall in two rounds, he must fall back on the diamond finesse.

Another possibility is to discard a heart on the king of clubs, then exit with a trump. The flaw in this plan is seen when the distribution is as follows:

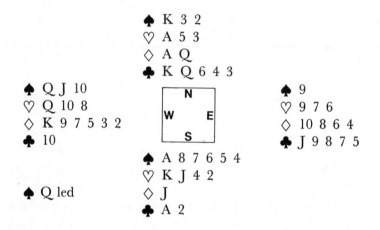

After king and ace of spades South plays ace of clubs, a club to the queen, and king of clubs, throwing a heart. If West does not ruff he is thrown in with a trump. Now West will assuredly lead a diamond and South will have to guess whether to finesse a diamond now or a heart later. This plan is inferior to playing off the top hearts, with the diamond finesse in reserve.

However, South can give himself two genuine chances by discarding the jack of diamonds on the third club. The difference is that when West comes in with a trump he cannot put the declarer to a premature guess. As the cards lie, he must present South with a free finesse in diamonds or must lead a heart into the K J.

Dealer, South   N–S vulnerable

```
                    ♠ 9 6 4
                    ♡ 6 3
                    ◇ J 8 5
                    ♣ A K J 9 4
     ♡ 10 led
                    ♠ A Q J
                    ♡ A Q 5
                    ◇ A 10 4 2
                    ♣ 10 8 2
```

South	West	North	East
1NT	2♡	3♡(1)	pass
3NT	pass	pass	pass

Final contract—3NT

(1) Opposite a 15–17 no trump, North has an awkward call. Three clubs would be purely competitive and so, in the modern style, would 2NT. It would not be unreasonable to bid 3NT, taking a chance on the hearts.

The early play

West leads the 10 of hearts, described as a "strong card," no doubt from K J 10 in this instance. How should South plan the play?

First look

If he takes the first trick South apparently has nine winners in the shape of two spades, two hearts, a diamond and four clubs. Meanwhile, however, he may need to lose the lead twice and West's heart suit represents a danger.

Problem No. 12

Did you, by any chance, see this as a simple exercise in driving out the entry of the danger hand? So it is, but there is a trap.

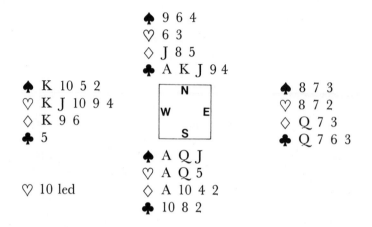

```
              ♠ 9 6 4
              ♡ 6 3
              ◊ J 8 5
              ♣ A K J 9 4
♠ K 10 5 2                        ♠ 8 7 3
♡ K J 10 9 4      N               ♡ 8 7 2
◊ K 9 6        W     E            ◊ Q 7 3
♣ 5               S              ♣ Q 7 6 3
              ♠ A Q J
              ♡ A Q 5
♡ 10 led      ◊ A 10 4 2
              ♣ 10 8 2
```

South is playing in 3NT after West has overcalled in hearts. South wins the heart lead and, with the correct notion of attacking West, the danger hand, crosses to ♣A for a spade finesse. West wins and clears the hearts. South wins the third round and leads the 10 of clubs.

If East wins this club trick, South has nine tricks, but East meanly holds off. South now can make only three tricks in clubs and finishes one down.

In seeking to establish a second spade trick, South has managed to destroy his own line of communication. It was right to play on spades first, but wrong to use a club to cross to dummy for this purpose. Instead, South should play the jack of spades from hand at trick two. Then he holds up the ace of hearts until the third round and runs the 10 of clubs. If East holds off, South can duck the second round as well.

Dealer, South   Neither side vulnerable

```
                    ♠ J 10 5
                    ♡ K 6 3
                    ◇ A 9 7 4 2
                    ♣ Q 6
♠ 9 led
                    ♠ A K 3
                    ♡ A J
                    ◇ K 8 3
                    ♣ A J 10 9 4
```

South	West	North	East
2NT	pass	3♣(1)	pass
3NT	pass	4NT(2)	pass
6NT(3)	pass	pass	pass

Final contract—6NT

(1) As three diamonds, in the system played, would have been a transfer to three hearts, North bids a Baron three clubs, asking partner to show 4-card suits "upwards."

(2) As it is unlikely there would be any advantage from playing in diamonds, North makes his slam try in notrumps.

(3) South accepts the invitation because good 5-card suits are a great asset in 6NT.

The early play

West leads the 9 of spades, dummy plays the 10 and East the 6. How should South plan the play?

First look

Now that South can count on three tricks in spades, five tricks in clubs would be enough for the slam. If the clubs don't perform, however, he will need to develop at least one trick elsewhere.

Problem No. 13

It is easy to form an inferior plan, based on the chances in clubs and diamonds. South may think: "I can lead the queen of clubs and, if this holds, finesse the 9. Then, before laying down the ace of clubs, I duck a diamond. If diamonds are 3–2 I'll make twelve tricks—even if East began with K x x x in clubs."

The weakness in this plan is that if the club finesse loses, the slam is almost sure to fail.

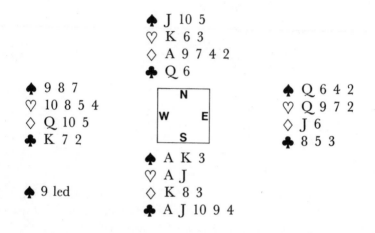

```
                    ♠ J 10 5
                    ♡ K 6 3
                    ◇ A 9 7 4 2
                    ♣ Q 6
  ♠ 9 8 7                              ♠ Q 6 4 2
  ♡ 10 8 5 4          N               ♡ Q 9 7 2
  ◇ Q 10 5        W       E           ◇ J 6
  ♣ K 7 2             S               ♣ 8 5 3
                    ♠ A K 3
  ♠ 9 led          ♡ A J
                    ◇ K 8 3
                    ♣ A J 10 9 4
```

South is in 6NT and West's spade lead is won by dummy's 10. If South finesses the queen of clubs and loses to the king on the first or second round, his prospects are slim. He can no longer afford to duck a diamond; he will lack entries to finesse the jack of hearts and make three tricks in that suit; and squeeze possibilities are remote.

South can give himself an appreciably better chance by finessing the jack of hearts at trick two. If this wins he can give up a club and be sure of twelve tricks. If the heart finesse loses, he can still try for five tricks in clubs. Thus declarer succeeds whenever East has the queen of hearts and also when East holds K x or K x x in clubs.

Dealer, North   Both sides vulnerable

♠ 10 5
♡ A Q 10 7 6 4
◇ Q
♣ A 7 4 2

♠ 7 led

♠ A Q 6
♡ 3
◇ A K 8 6 5 3 2
♣ Q 3

South	West	North	East
—	—	1♡	1♠
2◇	pass	2♡	pass
2♠	pass	3♣	pass
3NT(1)	pass	pass	pass

Final contract—3NT

(1) Six diamonds is a possible contract on the combined hands, especially after East's spade overcall, and South might have given it a chance by rebidding three diamonds at this point. North would then have been able to attach considerable value to his singleton queen.

The early play

West leads the 7 of spades, and as he must retain entry to his hand South does not hold up but takes the first trick with the queen. How should he continue?

First look

If diamonds are 3–2 there will be plenty of tricks, but life is not always like that.

Problem No. 14

The declarer's first instinct may be to cross to the queen of diamonds and return to the ace of spades to run the suit. If he places all his eggs in this basket he will go hungry.

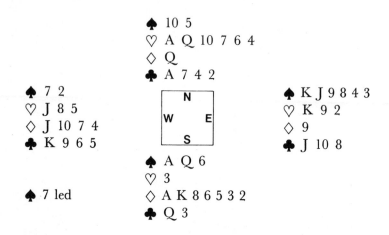

```
                    ♠ 10 5
                    ♡ A Q 10 7 6 4
                    ◇ Q
                    ♣ A 7 4 2
    ♠ 7 2                              ♠ K J 9 8 4 3
    ♡ J 8 5                            ♡ K 9 2
    ◇ J 10 7 4                         ◇ 9
    ♣ K 9 6 5                          ♣ J 10 8
                    ♠ A Q 6
                    ♡ 3
  ♠ 7 led          ◇ A K 8 6 5 3 2
                    ♣ Q 3
```

South plays in 3NT after East has overcalled in spades. West leads the 7 of spades, East plays the 8 and South wins at once, as he may need the ace of spades for entry.

Obviously it would be fatal, as the cards lie, to cross to the queen of diamonds and return to the ace of spades in the hope of running the diamonds. Since six tricks in diamonds will be more than enough for game, declarer should tackle this suit in a way that will leave him with other chances in the event of a bad break. After winning the first trick with the queen of spades he must play off ace and king of diamonds. If all follow, he gives up a diamond and still has the ace of spades as an entry.

As the cards lie, East discards on the second diamond, so South must now attempt to develop five tricks in hearts. As East on the bidding is sure to hold one of the side kings and may hold both, a finesse of the ♡10 is the best chance. This forces the king, and when the hearts later break 3–3 South has ten tricks by way of five hearts, two spades, two diamonds, and the ace of clubs.

Dealer, South   Both sides vulnerable

♠ A 10 8
♡ Q 9 4 3
◇ A 10 9 2
♣ 10 6

◇ K led

♠ K Q J
♡ A 10 8 6 5 2
◇ 7
♣ A Q J

South	West	North	East
1♡	pass	3♡	pass
4NT(1)	pass	5♡	pass
6♡	pass	pass	pass

Final contract—Six Hearts

(1) When partner raises one heart to three hearts, the hand looks very much like six hearts, but it is still advisable to check on aces. It is possible to construct shapely hands with no aces which would be worth a double raise.

The early play

West leads the king of diamonds, dummy wins with the ace, and East plays the 4. How should South plan the play?

First look

It looks as though South will need either a successful finesse in clubs or, if the club finesse is wrong, some luck in the trump suit.

Problem No. 15

With Q 9 x x opposite A 10 8 x x x there are two ways of making all the tricks: queen from dummy will gain if the defender on the left has a singleton jack, but ace first will gain when either opponent holds a singleton king. In general, therefore, ace first is the correct play. The result on this occasion was disappointing.

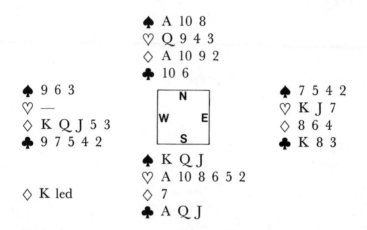

♠ A 10 8
♡ Q 9 4 3
◇ A 10 9 2
♣ 10 6

♠ 9 6 3
♡ —
◇ K Q J 5 3
♣ 9 7 5 4 2

♠ 7 5 4 2
♡ K J 7
◇ 8 6 4
♣ K 8 3

◇ K led

♠ K Q J
♡ A 10 8 6 5 2
◇ 7
♣ A Q J

Playing in six hearts, South won the diamond lead in dummy and played a heart to the ace. Later he found the club finesse right but two trump losers were inescapable.

"Couldn't you have made the safety play in trumps?" demanded North irritably.

"I know all about that," said South, "but how could I give up the chance of dropping a singleton king when there might have been a loser in clubs?"

Precisely! That is why the clubs should be tested first. When the club finesse holds, South's only problem is to avoid two losers in hearts. A low heart from hand is a perfect safety play against K J x in either defending hand.

3. Hidden Chances

The term "Hidden Chances" includes both safety plays that allow for hostile distribution and extra-chance plays that will provide some cover should the hand develop in an unpleasant way.

It wasn't easy to lose 6NT on the following deal, but South managed it.

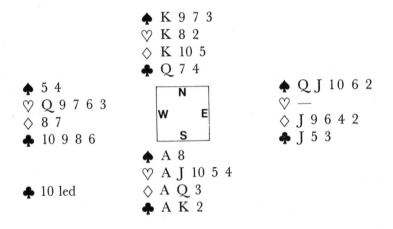

♠ K 9 7 3
♡ K 8 2
◇ K 10 5
♣ Q 7 4

♠ 5 4
♡ Q 9 7 6 3
◇ 8 7
♣ 10 9 8 6

♠ Q J 10 6 2
♡ —
◇ J 9 6 4 2
♣ J 5 3

♣ 10 led

♠ A 8
♡ A J 10 5 4
◇ A Q 3
♣ A K 2

West led the 10 of clubs against 6NT. "I won't keep you long over this," remarked the declarer, laying down the ace of hearts at trick two. When he discovered East's void he took a very long time indeed, but the contract eluded him. (It can be done at double-dummy: lead a spade to the A 8, forcing East to split, and subsequently end-play East in spades.)

Here the *only* danger was a 5–0 break in hearts. The safety play to be sure of four tricks in hearts is too rare to be in the textbooks, but it is not difficult to work out: lead low from dummy and put in the 10 whether East follows suit or shows out.

This is another hand that looked too easy:

```
                        ♠ A 6
                        ♡ J 8
                        ♦ 9 7 4 2
                        ♣ K Q 8 6 3
  ♠ 4                   ┌─────────┐      ♠ 10 9 8 5 2
  ♡ K Q 10 5 2         │    N    │      ♡ 9 6 3
  ♦ J 6 3              │ W     E │      ♦ 8
  ♣ 9 7 4 2            │    S    │      ♣ A J 10 5
                        └─────────┘
                        ♠ K Q J 7 3
                        ♡ A 7 4
  ♡ K led               ♦ A K Q 10 5
                        ♣ —
```

Playing in six diamonds, South wins the heart lead and draws trumps in three rounds. He leads a spade to the ace and returns a spade, discovering the 5–1 break. Suddenly the contract is impossible. Declarer can throw a heart on the next spade, but he is left with three losers and only one trump in dummy. He can no longer take advantage of the position of the ace of clubs.

The right play here is to draw three trumps, then test the spade situation by playing king and another. Finding the 5–1 break, South wins the spade ace and takes the ruffing finesse in clubs to establish his twelfth trick. He gives up one heart, ruffs a heart, and disposes of his spade loser on the queen of clubs.

Here the play that provides the extra chance is more difficult to foresee:

```
  ♠ 6 4 3 2                       ♠ A K J 9 7 5
  ♡ A Q 10                        ♡ J
  ♦ A 5 3                         ♦ K Q 4
  ♣ J 10 4                        ♣ A K 2
                   ♦ J led
```

Playing in six spades, East wins the diamond lead and discovers on the first round of trumps that South started with Q 10 8 of spades. If he cashes the top diamonds and then gives South the lead in trumps, South will exit with a heart and East will not know whether to finesse in this suit or in clubs. He can make sure of the contract by cashing the ace of hearts after clearing the diamonds. Now the throw-in on the third round of trumps end-plays South.

Dealer, South   Both sides vulnerable

```
              ♠ Q 10 6 3
              ♡ A K 8 7
              ◇ Q 7 4 2
              ♣ K
♡ Q led

              ♠ K J 8
              ♡ 5
              ◇ A 9 6 5 3
              ♣ A 9 8 4
```

South	West	North	East
1 ◇	pass	1 ♡	pass
1NT	pass	3NT(1)	pass
pass	pass		

Final contract—3NT

(1) After South's rebid of 1NT there seems little point in exploring other possibilities.

The early play

West leads the queen of hearts. As he would not relish a switch to clubs, declarer decides to win. At trick two he plays a spade to the king and ace. West leads the jack of hearts, which is allowed to hold, then plays a low club to dummy's king. East has played the 2 and 4 of hearts. How should South plan the rest of the play?

First look

South can count eight top tricks. As the clubs are now wide open except for the ace, he cannot afford to lose two diamonds.

Problem No. 16

There are two important questions: who has the king of diamonds and what is the best way to attack the suit?

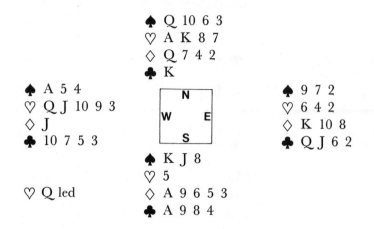

♠ Q 10 6 3
♡ A K 8 7
◇ Q 7 4 2
♣ K

♠ A 5 4
♡ Q J 10 9 3
◇ J
♣ 10 7 5 3

♠ 9 7 2
♡ 6 4 2
◇ K 10 8
♣ Q J 6 2

♡ Q led

♠ K J 8
♡ 5
◇ A 9 6 5 3
♣ A 9 8 4

South is in 3NT and West leads the queen of hearts. Dummy wins and a spade is led to the king and ace. West leads the jack of hearts, which is allowed to hold, and then switches to a low club.

West's opening lead was in a suit bid by dummy, so presumably he has both length and a strong sequence. His failure to continue hearts, clearing the suit, suggests that either (a) he does not hold the king of diamonds, or possibly (b) that he has the king singleton and does not want to encourage South to lay down the ace.

It would be a mistake to play diamonds in the orthodox way—ace and another. As the cards lie, a lead of the queen from dummy, to be followed by a finesse against the 10, would succeed.

However, that is not quite the best answer. As West might hold a singleton king, it is slightly better to lead a low diamond from hand. When the jack is covered by the queen and king, South plans later to finesse the 9. He will have taken a wrong view of the diamonds only if West holds precisely J 10 alone.

Dealer, West   Neither side vulnerable

♠ K 6 3
♥ J 4 2
♦ K J 8 6
♣ 7 5 3

♣ K led

♠ A 7 5
♥ A K Q 10 8
♦ A 7
♣ J 8 2

South	West	North	East
—	pass	pass	pass
1 ♥	1 ♠	dble (1)	pass
3 ♥ (2)	pass	4 ♥	pass
pass	pass		

Final contract—Four Hearts

(1) A negative double, indicating moderate values.

(2) At this point two spades, a bid of the opponent's suit, would have been a slightly better choice, because the hand might play better in notrump.

The early play

West begins with king, ace and another club, East winning with the queen. East returns the 10 of spades. South wins with the ace and all follow to two rounds of trumps. How should South continue?

First look

Having lost three clubs already, South is a trick short. He cannot be hopeful of the diamond finesse, because West passed originally, has overcalled in spades, and has produced ace and king of clubs. To find West with 10 9 of diamonds precisely, allowing a ruffing finesse against the queen, is a slim chance.

Problem No. 17

South does not need to find West with exactly 10 9 of diamonds: any doubleton including the 10 or 9 will be good enough.

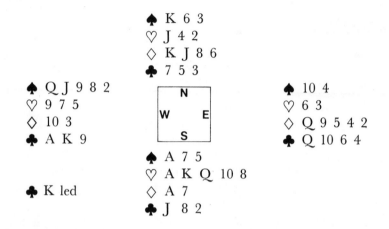

♠ K 6 3
♡ J 4 2
◇ K J 8 6
♣ 7 5 3

♠ Q J 9 8 2
♡ 9 7 5
◇ 10 3
♣ A K 9

♠ 10 4
♡ 6 3
◇ Q 9 5 4 2
♣ Q 10 6 4

♣ K led

♠ A 7 5
♡ A K Q 10 8
◇ A 7
♣ J 8 2

South plays in four hearts after West, who passed originally, has overcalled in spades. The defenders begin with three rounds of clubs. East wins the third round and switches to the 10 of spades.

As West can hardly have the queen of diamonds in addition to the values he has shown, South wins the third round of trumps in dummy and leads the jack of diamonds, forcing a cover from East. South wins with the ace and leads the 7 to the king, on which West's 10 appears. Now the 8 6 of diamonds are equals against East's 9 and a ruffing finesse establishes the tenth trick.

On the third round of diamonds it is certainly better to play East for the 9 than to play for West to hold 10 9 x precisely, both on general grounds and because West, who bid spades, has already shown six cards in hearts and clubs. He could hardly have overcalled in spades on Q J x x.

Dealer, North   Game all

```
                        ♠ A K Q
                        ♡ J 7 6 4
                        ◇ K 7 5
                        ♣ K J 8
   ♠ 10 led

                        ♠ 5
                        ♡ A Q 2
                        ◇ A 6 4
                        ♣ Q 10 9 7 6 5
```

South	West	North	East
—	—	1NT	pass
2♣(1)	pass	2♡	pass
3♣	pass	3♠(2)	pass
4♣	pass	4◇	pass
6♣	pass	pass	pass

Final contract—Six Clubs

(1) South is playing the style in which any new suit at the three level, following a Stayman two clubs, is forcing to game.

(2) The Stayman concept has now been abandoned. North is showing a control in spades and willingness to advance in clubs.

The early play

West leads the 10 of spades to dummy's ace. How should South plan the play?

First look

The spades will provide two discards, but South will still be one trick short of the slam.

Problem No. 18

South had a plan. If West held the king of hearts and A x of clubs, and if he ducked the first club, he might be thrown in later to make a disadvantageous lead.

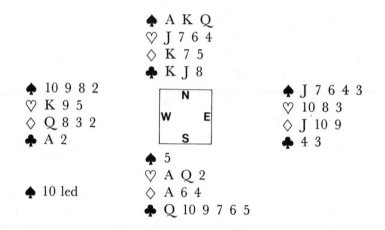

♠ A K Q
♡ J 7 6 4
◇ K 7 5
♣ K J 8

♠ 10 9 8 2
♡ K 9 5
◇ Q 8 3 2
♣ A 2

♠ J 7 6 4 3
♡ 10 8 3
◇ J 10 9
♣ 4 3

♠ 5
♡ A Q 2
◇ A 6 4
♣ Q 10 9 7 6 5

♠ 10 led

Playing in six clubs, South won the spade lead in dummy, came to hand with the ace of diamonds, and led a mildly deceptive 10 of clubs. It can be seen that if West lets this pass he can be end-played later. South eliminates spades and diamonds before leading a second round of clubs. West, in with the ace of clubs, is forced to lead a heart into the A Q or concede a ruff-and-discard.

For this plan to succeed, West must hold precisely A x in clubs and must duck the first round of clubs, but no good player, hoping to make a trick with the king of hearts, would leave himself with a bare ace of trumps.

A better line, somehow elusive, is to play for the drop of the king of hearts in three rounds. To prepare for this, declarer must play off the top spades, discarding two hearts, lead a heart to the ace, and then a trump to West's ace. He has enough entries now to ruff two hearts and return to dummy to make his twelfth trick with the jack of hearts. This line, as compared with the straightforward finesse of the queen, loses only when East holds at least four hearts to the king; it gains whenever West holds K x x or K x or singleton king, a much superior chance.

Dealer, South   Both sides vulnerable

<pre>
                    ♠ 6 5 2
                    ♡ 10 9 4
                    ◇ J 7 3
                    ♣ A 6 5 3
    ♠ J led
                    ♠ A Q
                    ♡ A J 3
                    ◇ A 10 6 2
                    ♣ K Q 10 4
</pre>

South	West	North	East
South	*West*	*North*	*East*
2NT (1)	pass	3NT	pass
pass	pass		

Final contract—3NT

(1) Not the greatest of 2NT openings, with 6 out of 20 points wrapped up in the unaccompanied A Q of spades, but the hand contains fair intermediates and tenaces in every suit.

The early play

West leads the jack of spades, East plays the 7 and South the queen. How should South plan the play?

First look

So long as the clubs are not particularly hostile, there are eight tricks in sight, with possibilities of a ninth in both hearts and diamonds. The problem is how to combine the various chances.

Problem No. 19

The normal way to play the clubs would be king, then low to the ace, so that J x x x in the East hand could be picked up. However, the most likely chance for a ninth trick on this deal appears to lie in hearts, where two finesses can be taken. South may therefore decide to play the clubs in a way likely to create two entries for heart finesses.

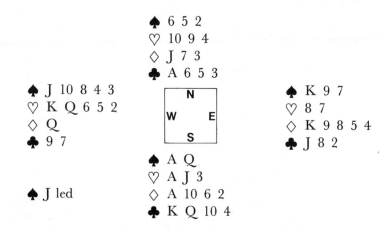

```
                    ♠ 6 5 2
                    ♡ 10 9 4
                    ◇ J 7 3
                    ♣ A 6 5 3
♠ J 10 8 4 3      ┌─────────┐      ♠ K 9 7
♡ K Q 6 5 2       │    N    │      ♡ 8 7
◇ Q               │ W     E │      ◇ K 9 8 5 4
♣ 9 7             │    S    │      ♣ J 8 2
                  └─────────┘
♠ J led             ♠ A Q
                    ♡ A J 3
                    ◇ A 10 6 2
                    ♣ K Q 10 4
```

Playing in 3NT, South wins the spade lead and plays king and queen of clubs. When all follow, he overtakes the 10 with the ace and runs the 10 of hearts. West's queen wins and he clears the spades. Declarer crosses to the 6 of clubs for another heart finesse, but he is unlucky. Both hearts are wrong and the defenders make three more tricks in spades.

The play of the clubs was sound enough, but declarer missed a minute extra chance. It costs nothing to lay down the ace of diamonds at an early stage. If a singleton king or queen falls (or there is a doubleton K Q) the ninth trick can be safely established.

The same sort of play, in similar circumstances, can be made with a weaker holding, such as A J x x opposite 10 x. There is no danger that the opponents will be able to run four tricks in the suit when they gain the lead.

Dealer, West   N–S vulnerable

♠ 9 6 4 3
♡ K 9 8 5
◇ 6 3
♣ A Q J

♡ J led

♠ A Q 8 2
♡ A Q 10 7 6 4 2
◇ A Q
♣ —

South	West	North	East
—	1◇	pass	pass
dble	pass	1♠(1)	pass
4♡	pass	6♡	pass
pass	pass		

Final contract—Six Hearts

(1) One heart would have been better at this stage, because after one spade a good heart fit might be lost.

The early play

West leads the jack of hearts and East follows suit. How should South plan the play?

First look

No doubt West has the three missing kings and there are several ways of forcing him to lead from one of them. But that will be declarer's eleventh trick, not his twelfth.

Problem No. 20

After a frustrating search for an end-play that will produce not one extra trick, but two, South may decide in the end to play West for a doubleton king of spades. He will have no success when the cards lie as follows:

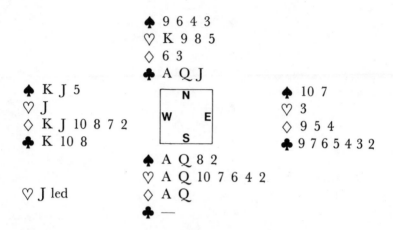

♠ 9 6 4 3
♡ K 9 8 5
♢ 6 3
♣ A Q J

♠ K J 5
♡ J
♢ K J 10 8 7 2
♣ K 10 8

♠ 10 7
♡ 3
♢ 9 5 4
♣ 9 7 6 5 4 3 2

♠ A Q 8 2
♡ A Q 10 7 6 4 2
♢ A Q
♣ —

♡ J led

It is easy to overlook a line of play that will win unless West has as many as four spades. The general plan is to discard three spades from the South hand and establish a long spade in dummy.

South wins West's singleton trump lead with the king of hearts, plays ace of clubs, discarding a spade, then queen of clubs, discarding another spade. West cannot do better than exit with a third club, on which South discards the queen of spades. Now declarer can cash the ace of spades and use the three trump entries on the table to ruff two spades and return to make the fourth spade, which will provide a discard for the queen of diamonds.

Dealer, South   Neither side vulnerable

                   ♠ Q 5
                   ♡ A J 9 3
                   ◇ 10 7
                   ♣ K J 10 7 6

♡ K led

                   ♠ A K 9 8 7 6 4
                   ♡ 10
                   ◇ A K Q 9
                   ♣ 5

South	*West*	*North*	*East*
2♠	pass	3♣	pass
3♠	pass	4♡(1)	pass
5◇(2)	pass	6♠	pass
pass	pass		

Final contract—Six Spades

(1) North is not bidding hearts as a suit, but is showing a control on the way to six spades.

(2) Preferable to a Blackwood 4NT, because it gives partner more chance to express his values. If South bids 4NT and North shows the number of aces he holds, South will still not know whether the spades are solid.

The early play

West leads the king of hearts, dummy plays the ace and East the 5. How should South plan the play?

First look

With a certain loser in clubs, South must assume that the spades are not 4–0. He still needs to take care of the fourth round of diamonds.

Problem No. 21

This deal from a pairs contest shows how easy it is to overlook the value of two cards that are "equals" against an opposing winner.

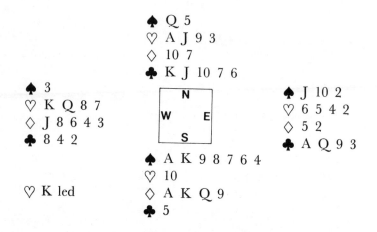

```
                    ♠ Q 5
                    ♡ A J 9 3
                    ◇ 10 7
                    ♣ K J 10 7 6
  ♠ 3                            ♠ J 10 2
  ♡ K Q 8 7        N             ♡ 6 5 4 2
  ◇ J 8 6 4 3    W   E           ◇ 5 2
  ♣ 8 4 2          S             ♣ A Q 9 3
                    ♠ A K 9 8 7 6 4
                    ♡ 10
  ♡ K led           ◇ A K Q 9
                    ♣ 5
```

When West led the king of hearts against six spades, several declarers won with the ace, came to hand with a diamond, and tried a club finesse. This lost and East returned a heart. South ruffed, played a spade to the queen, then attempted to ruff the third round of diamonds. East overruffed the dummy and the contract was one down.

South had overlooked the combined value of the jack and 9 of hearts. At trick two he should lead the jack of hearts from dummy and discard his losing club. West wins and will probably exit with a club. South ruffs, draws two trumps with the ace and queen, then leads the 9 of hearts, discarding the 9 of diamonds. This line will fail only if hearts are 6–2 and trumps 3–1. Obviously, there is a greater danger that the diamonds will be 5–2 than the hearts 6–2.

Dealer, North   Neither side vulnerable

♠ J 4
♡ 10 5 3
◇ A 10
♣ A Q 9 7 4 2

♠ 3 led

♠ K 8 5 2
♡ A 7 4 2
◇ K 6 4 3
♣ K

South	West	North	East
—	—	1♣	pass
1◇	pass	2♣	pass
2NT(1)	pass	3NT (2)	pass
pass	pass		

Final contract—3NT

(1) On the cautious side, but the lack of good intermediates and the singleton in clubs are discouraging factors.

(2) North has a minimum opening, but such hands tend to develop seven tricks or nine, according to whether the long suit can be set up in time.

The early play

West leads the 3 of spades, South plays low from dummy, and East plays the queen. How should South plan the play? (West drops the 5 on the first round of clubs.)

First look

If clubs are 3–3, or there is a doubleton J 10, South can run ten tricks. However, the cards may not lie so well.

Problem No. 22

Nothing would be gained by holding off the first trick, and a switch to hearts would be unwelcome. So South wins with the king of spades, then leads the king of clubs, on which West drops the 5. If South plays low from dummy he will be dependent on the clubs breaking 3–3 (or there being a doubleton J 10). He can give himself additional chances by overtaking the king with the ace. The cards may lie like this:

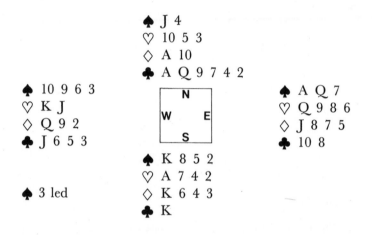

♠ J 4
♡ 10 5 3
◇ A 10
♣ A Q 9 7 4 2

♠ 10 9 6 3
♡ K J
◇ Q 9 2
♣ J 6 5 3

♠ A Q 7
♡ Q 9 8 6
◇ J 8 7 5
♣ 10 8

♠ K 8 5 2
♡ A 7 4 2
◇ K 6 4 3
♣ K

♠ 3 led

West leads the 3 of spades against 3NT, East plays the queen (normally correct from his holding) and South wins. He overtakes the king of clubs with the ace and leads the queen. The 9 7 are then equals against West's J 6 and after he knocks out West's stopper he still has the diamond ace as entry for the established clubs. The defenders are held to three tricks in spades and one in clubs.

This line of play gains when East has a doubleton J 8 or 10 8 and will go amiss only if clubs are 3–3 and the defenders are able to take four spade tricks when they gain the lead. This could happen only if West had made the strange lead of the 3 from a holding such as A 10 9 6 3.

If the clubs are 4–2 and the doubleton does not include two of the higher cards, the contract can never be made. The overtaking play will mean, perhaps, three down instead of two down.

Dealer, South   Both sides vulnerable

                   ♠ K 10 4
                   ♡ A K J 9 5 3
                   ◇ 6
                   ♣ 10 4 2

♡ 10 led

                   ♠ A J 8
                   ♡ 7 6 4
                   ◇ A K J 8
                   ♣ A Q 6

South	*West*	*North*	*East*
1 ◇	pass	1 ♡	pass
3NT(1)	pass	6NT(2)	pass
pass	pass		

Final contract—6NT

(1) Whether South should rebid 2NT or 3NT is a question of system.

(2) There are other ways of advancing, obviously, but the direct way is often best, and there is no reason to suppose that six hearts would be a better contract than 6NT, with the lead coming up to the strong hand.

The early play

West leads the 10 of hearts, the king wins, and South is pleased to see the queen fall on the next round. How should he continue?

First look

With the hearts dividing, there are eleven tricks on top. The odds are at least 3–1 that South will make the contract, as he can take two finesses in turn. But perhaps he can improve on that.

Problem No. 23

It is the sort of hand where some players lead out the long suit, embarrassing themselves instead of the opposition, and end up by taking two finesses, which both lose. There is a better way!

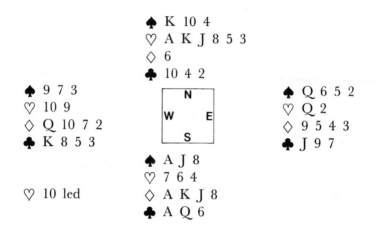

♠ K 10 4
♡ A K J 8 5 3
◇ 6
♣ 10 4 2

♠ 9 7 3
♡ 10 9
◇ Q 10 7 2
♣ K 8 5 3

N
W   E
S

♠ Q 6 5 2
♡ Q 2
◇ 9 5 4 3
♣ J 9 7

♡ 10 led

♠ A J 8
♡ 7 6 4
◇ A K J 8
♣ A Q 6

South is in 6NT and West, not wanting to assist the declarer in any way, leads the 10 of hearts. A second round of hearts drops the queen.

At this point South can make a certainty of the contract by the simple stratagem of leading a diamond from dummy and putting in the 8 unless East inserts a high card. When West wins the trick, any return will be to declarer's advantage.

If East plays the 9 or 10 of diamonds on the first round South will simply cover with the jack. If it holds, declarer has his twelfth trick. If it loses to the queen, declarer's A K 8 will now be a major tenace. Whatever West returns will give South his twelfth trick.

Dealer, South   Both sides vulnerable

<pre>
                    ♠ J 9 6
                    ♡ 7 5 4 2
                    ◇ A Q 10
                    ♣ Q 5 3
♠ 5 led
                    ♠ Q 4
                    ♡ A Q J 9 3
                    ◇ K 8 4
                    ♣ A 10 7
</pre>

South	West	North	East
1NT(1)	pass	2NT(2)	pass
3NT	pass	pass	pass

Final contract—3NT

(1) The opening bid of 1NT has many merits as compared with one heart: it is descriptive; you avoid the awkward situation where partner responds 1NT to an opening one heart; concealment of the five-card major may work to your advantage in the play; and you make it more difficult for West to compete in spades.

(2) The raise is on the basis of a 15–17 notrump.

The early play

West leads the 5 of spades and dummy's 9 is covered by the 10 and queen. How should South plan the play?

First look

Declarer notes, first, that although there are nine hearts in the two hands, 3NT is at least as good a contract as four hearts. However, the spades are probably 5–3 or 6–2, so South cannot afford to lose the lead.

Problem No. 24

There is no good reason for South to reject the heart finesse. If the king is wrong he will go down at once, but if East has K x or K x x he will make the contract easily. But another possibility must be considered: suppose East has K 10 x x?

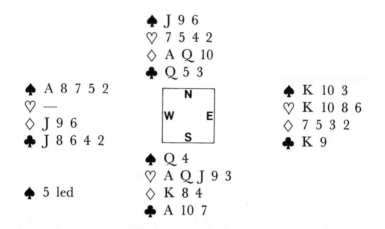

```
              ♠ J 9 6
              ♡ 7 5 4 2
              ◇ A Q 10
              ♣ Q 5 3

♠ A 8 7 5 2        N         ♠ K 10 3
♡ —           W         E    ♡ K 10 8 6
◇ J 9 6            S         ◇ 7 5 3 2
♣ J 8 6 4 2                  ♣ K 9

♠ 5 led       ♠ Q 4
              ♡ A Q J 9 3
              ◇ K 8 4
              ♣ A 10 7
```

South plays 3NT and West's lead of the 5 of spades is covered by the 9, 10 and queen. Clearly declarer cannot afford to lose the lead in hearts, as the opponents will surely be able to cash four or five spade tricks.

To pick up the hearts without loss when the cards lie as above, South will need three entries to dummy. Since two diamond tricks will be enough for game, assuming that five tricks can be made in hearts, South should begin by overtaking the king of diamonds with the ace. He finesses the jack of hearts and West discards a club. Now a finesse of the 10 of diamonds will create an extra entry to the table and South will end up with ten tricks.

To begin with a low diamond to the queen is not so good, because West may be smart enough to insert the jack on the next round, blocking the entry-finesse.

Dealer, West   Neither side vulnerable

<pre>
                    ♠ K 10 6 2
                    ♡ 10 6 4 2
                    ◇ 7 5 3
                    ♣ A 8
     ♣ K led
                    ♠ Q 4
                    ♡ A K J 9 7 3
                    ◇ K J
                    ♣ 9 5 4
</pre>

South	West	North	East
—	1♠	pass	pass
3♡(1)	pass	4♡	pass
pass	pass		

Final contract—Four Hearts

(1) South is a trifle strong for a simple two hearts in the protective position. The jump to three hearts signifies no more than the values for an opening bid with a good six-card suit.

The early play

West leads the king of clubs. Despite the slight risk of ace of spades and a spade ruff, South plays low from dummy to prevent East from gaining the lead in clubs at any time. West continues with a low club to the ace, East completing an echo of the 6 and 2. All follow to the first round of hearts. How should South continue?

First look

South has three top losers—one in spades, one in diamonds and one in clubs. He must either find the diamond queen with East or develop an extra trick in spades.

Problem No. 25

As West has opened one spade, it seems a better chance to find him with the jack of spades than to find East with the queen of diamonds. However, a straightforward finesse of the 10 of spades on the second round of the suit may prove disappointing.

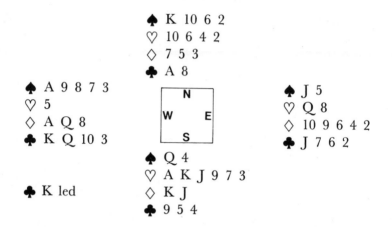

♠ K 10 6 2
♡ 10 6 4 2
♢ 7 5 3
♣ A 8

♠ A 9 8 7 3
♡ 5
♢ A Q 8
♣ K Q 10 3

♠ J 5
♡ Q 8
♢ 10 9 6 4 2
♣ J 7 6 2

♠ Q 4
♡ A K J 9 7 3
♢ K J
♣ 9 5 4

♣ K led

South plays in four hearts after West has opened one spade. West leads the king of clubs and is allowed to hold the trick. West continues with a low club to dummy's ace, and all follow to a round of trumps.

Suppose that South ruffs a club, returns to the king of hearts, and leads the queen of spades. West will win and exit with a low spade. It is natural to finesse the 10 and the result is two down.

To find East with the doubleton jack of spades is annoying, but South can guard against this possibility. After eliminating the clubs he should lead a low spade from hand, not the queen. The king wins and a spade is returned. As the cards lie, the jack falls, establishing dummy's 10 for a diamond discard. And if West began with A J x x x of spades? Then he will be on play when he wins with the ace, forced to concede a trick whether he leads a spade, a diamond or a club.

4. Placement

Bridge would be a dull game, or at any rate a very different game, if it were not for the rule that the player who has won a trick must lead to the next trick. Many of the commonest, and also the most perplexing, plays in the game occur in the field of communication. Such plays are equally critical for defenders and attackers.

Sometimes the declarer is concerned with organizing his own entries satisfactorily; sometimes he is thinking more about preventing a particular opponent from gaining the lead. We will begin with two examples of the first kind, where the declarer must make the best use of his own entries.

♠ K Q 6 2
♡ K
◇ K J 6 4
♣ A J 10 4

♠ J led

♠ A 4 3
♡ A 10 9 8 7
◇ A 8
♣ 6 5 2

South plays in 3NT and West leads the jack of spades. The contract cannot fail so long as South concentrates on making his ninth trick in hearts. If he wins the spade lead in dummy, cashes the king of hearts, and crosses to one of his aces, he will find that he cannot establish extra tricks in hearts (unless the queen or jack falls on the first or second round). He has six top tricks outside hearts and needs only to develop three tricks in this suit. He can do this by winning the spade lead in dummy, overtaking the king of hearts with the ace, and continuing the suit. In due course he will force out the queen and jack and he has sufficient entries to cash the established tricks, however the cards lie.

In the next example South plays in a suit contract and needs to develop just one extra trick in either hearts or clubs:

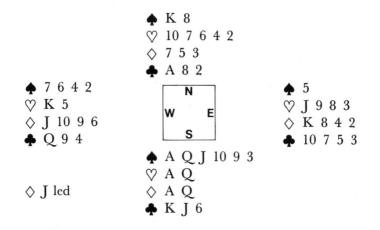

♠ K 8
♡ 10 7 6 4 2
◊ 7 5 3
♣ A 8 2

♠ 7 6 4 2
♡ K 5
◊ J 10 9 6
♣ Q 9 4

N
W E
S

♠ 5
♡ J 9 8 3
◊ K 8 4 2
♣ 10 7 5 3

◊ J led

♠ A Q J 10 9 3
♡ A Q
◊ A Q
♣ K J 6

South is in six spades, and one of his worries disappears when West leads the jack of diamonds. Now many players would cross to dummy for a heart finesse. This loses and West plays a trump. Now South needs to find the hearts 3–3 or, failing that, the queen of clubs on the right side. When all these chances fail, he remarks how unlucky he has been.

But it's not all bad luck. The contract is a lay-down so long as hearts are not worse than 4–2. Having won the first trick with the queen of diamonds, South must play ace and queen of hearts, clearing the decks for the establishment of a long heart. Say that the defenders win and play a trump, won in dummy. South ruffs a heart, returns to the king of spades, and ruffs another heart. Then he draws trumps and the ace of clubs is an entry for the fifth heart.

Problems where the object is to prevent a particular opponent from gaining the lead are still more frequent. These are a few positions in a single suit where the correct play is commonly missed:

7 6 2

J 8 4   Q 10

A K 9 5 3

Suppose that South wishes to establish this suit without

letting West into the lead. It is not good enough to lay down the ace, intending to cross to dummy for the next lead, because East may unblock the queen on the first round. If entries permit, South should lead from dummy on the first round and again on the second round. When the queen appears, it is allowed to hold.

A 10 8 6 5 2

Q   J 9 3

K 7 4

Here the aim is to keep East out of the lead. Suppose you make the first lead from dummy. When East puts in the 9, South must win, because East might hold Q 9 or J 9; now East will win the third round of the suit. The best line is to begin with a low card from hand. When West, perforce, plays the queen, South leaves him in possession.

This is another position worth remembering:

K Q 9 7 4 2

J   10 8 6 5

A 3

South wants to develop this suit without letting East into the lead. If entries permit, he should begin with a low card from hand; when the jack appears, he can duck.

In notrump contracts, especially, the early play is often determined by entry considerations. This is not a difficult hand, but the declarer must be awake:

♠ 10 6 4
♡ A Q
◇ K 8 4 2
♣ A J 7 2

♡ 5 led

♠ A J
♡ J 9 4
◇ A 10 3
♣ K 10 9 5 3

You are playing 3NT and West leads the 5 of hearts. First, it would be a mistake to finesse, because a spade return from East might establish three or four tricks for the defenders. You must go up with the ace of hearts, cash the ace of clubs and, if necessary, finesse in clubs towards West. You don't mind West winning a club trick, because with West on lead you have a double stop in spades. If West makes a neutral return you can establish your ninth trick by forcing out the king of hearts.

This is a more advanced exercise in the art of placement:

♠ K 8 5
♡ K J 9 8 5 4 2
♢ J 9 4
♣ —

♣ 6 led

♠ 6 4 3
♡ A Q 10 7
♢ A K 10 8
♣ Q 5

You are in four hearts and the 6 of clubs is led. How can you avoid the possible loss of a diamond and three spades? Simply discard a diamond from dummy on the opening lead! East, the non-danger hand, will win. When you have drawn trumps and ruffed the second club you play off two top diamonds and run the 8. Nothing can go wrong. If East wins the trick he must either attack spades from his side or allow you to discard another spade on the 10 of diamonds.

Dealer, North   Neither side vulnerable

```
                    ♠ 7 4
                    ♡ A K J 3
                    ◇ K J 3
                    ♣ A K 7 3
◇ Q led
                    ♠ K 8
                    ♡ Q 10 9 7 6 4
                    ◇ 10
                    ♣ 10 8 6 2
```

South	West	North	East
—	—	1 ♣	1 ◇
1 ♡	pass	3 ♡ (1)	pass
4 ♡ (2)	pass	pass	pass

Final contract—Four Hearts

(1) North may regret that he did not open one heart, as he now has an awkward call. He may feel that 3NT would be a safer spot, because of the threat of a diamond lead through the K J x in a heart contract, but the natural action is to support hearts.

(2) Fortunately South is short in diamonds and his distribution justifies a raise to game.

The early play

West leads the queen of diamonds. How should South plan the play?

First look

Given time, there are ten probable tricks in the two hands, but the ace of spades may be on the wrong side. South is in danger of losing a diamond, two spades and a club.

Problem No. 26

When the queen of diamonds was led, South automatically reached for the king. This turned out to be a fatal error, for the full hand was:

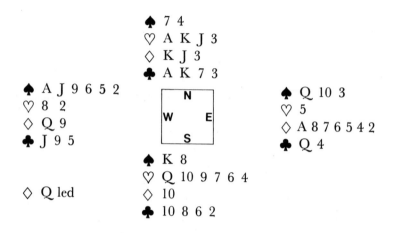

```
                      ♠ 7 4
                      ♡ A K J 3
                      ◇ K J 3
                      ♣ A K 7 3
  ♠ A J 9 6 5 2          N           ♠ Q 10 3
  ♡ 8 2           W           E      ♡ 5
  ◇ Q 9                               ◇ A 8 7 6 5 4 2
  ♣ J 9 5               S             ♣ Q 4
                      ♠ K 8
                      ♡ Q 10 9 7 6 4
  ◇ Q led            ◇ 10
                      ♣ 10 8 6 2
```

East covered the king of diamonds with the ace and fired back a spade. The defenders cashed two spades and exited with a trump. South was able to discard one club on the jack of diamonds but there was no way to escape a club loser.

South makes the contract easily so long as he refrains from covering the queen of diamonds at trick one. Two possibilities arise:

One, the queen of diamonds is allowed to hold. South later establishes a diamond trick by a ruffing finesse and discards a spade on the diamond winner. He can then afford to give up a club. He will lose one diamond, one club and one spade.

Two, East decides to overtake the queen of diamonds and lead a spade. South will lose the first three tricks, but now the K J of diamonds will be available for two club discards.

Dealer, West   N–S vulnerable

> ♠ K 6 2
> ♡ Q 10 7 3
> ◇ 7 5 4
> ♣ K J 3

♣ 10 led

> ♠ —
> ♡ A K 9 8 6 4 2
> ◇ A Q 6
> ♣ A 6 2

South	West	North	East
South	*West*	*North*	*East*
—	1♠	pass	2♠
4♡	4♠	5♡(1)	pass
pass(2)	pass		

Final contract—Five Hearts

(1) Obviously North could double four spades, but with a partner who has bid four hearts on his own, vulnerable, eleven tricks should be safe.

(2) South's hand is tempting, but he must remember that he has already made a big bid and his partner may be competing on a fairly weak hand.

The early play

West leads the 10 of clubs. How should South plan the play?

First look

South may be glad he kept his head, for there are three possible losers—two in diamonds and one in clubs. The first question is whether or not to take the free finesse offered by the lead of a club.

Problem No. 27

As West opened the bidding, and probably does not hold the queen of clubs, he is likely to hold both ace of spades and king of diamonds. Declarer's objective is to bring about a situation in which West will be forced to lead a diamond or concede a ruff-and-discard.

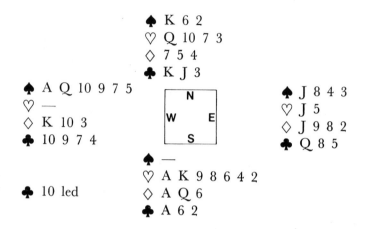

```
                    ♠ K 6 2
                    ♡ Q 10 7 3
                    ◇ 7 5 4
                    ♣ K J 3
♠ A Q 10 9 7 5         ┌─────────┐      ♠ J 8 4 3
♡ —                    │    N    │      ♡ J 5
◇ K 10 3               │ W     E │      ◇ J 9 8 2
♣ 10 9 7 4             │    S    │      ♣ Q 8 5
                       └─────────┘
                    ♠ —
                    ♡ A K 9 8 6 4 2
♣ 10 led            ◇ A Q 6
                    ♣ A 6 2
```

South plays in five hearts after West has opened one spade. West leads the 10 of clubs. As South wants to prevent East from gaining the lead at any point to play a diamond through the A Q, South's first move is to duck the 10 of clubs in both hands. West cannot do better than lead another club, which South wins in hand.

Preparing a throw-in, South plays ace of hearts and a heart to the queen, ruffs a spade and leads a third heart to dummy's 10. A second spade ruff is followed by a club to the king. Now declarer leads the king of spades from dummy and discards a low diamond. West wins and has no safe card of exit.

Dealer, South   Neither side vulnerable

♠ 9 7 2
♡ J 9 7 3
◇ A 10 6
♣ J 8 5

♣ K led

♠ A J 10 8
♡ A K 10 6 4
◇ K Q 7
♣ 2

South	West	North	East
1♡	pass	1NT(1)	pass
2♠	pass	4♡(2)	pass
pass	pass		

Final contract—Four Hearts

(1) A raise to two hearts would certainly not be wrong, but 1NT is sometimes preferred with 4–3–3–3 distribution.

(2) If he has any doubt about the jump to game, North should reflect that he might have raised to two hearts initially and that his partner, who has reversed over 1NT, would certainly have jumped to four hearts.

The early play

West begins with king and ace of clubs. South ruffs and lays down the ace of hearts, to which all follow. How should he continue?

First look

If things go badly, South may lose a club, a heart and two spades. There are slight problems both of entry and control.

Problem No. 28

If South plays off a second top heart and fails to drop the queen, the hand may turn awkward.

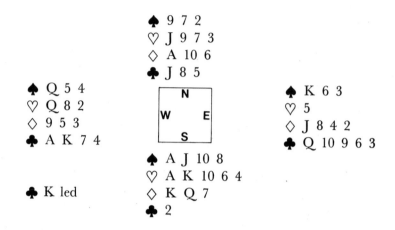

```
                    ♠ 9 7 2
                    ♡ J 9 7 3
                    ◇ A 10 6
                    ♣ J 8 5
  ♠ Q 5 4            ┌─────────┐      ♠ K 6 3
  ♡ Q 8 2            │    N    │      ♡ 5
  ◇ 9 5 3            │ W     E │      ◇ J 8 4 2
  ♣ A K 7 4          │    S    │      ♣ Q 10 9 6 3
                    └─────────┘
                    ♠ A J 10 8
  ♣ K led           ♡ A K 10 6 4
                    ◇ K Q 7
                    ♣ 2
```

Suppose that South, playing in four hearts, ruffs the second round of clubs and plays off ace and king of hearts. When the queen does not drop, he enters dummy with the ace of diamonds and runs the 9 of spades, losing to the queen. West cashes the queen of hearts and leads another club, which takes the declarer's last trump. Now South is foolishly locked in his own hand, with no chance to take a second finesse in spades.

From the beginning, the declarer should place his faith in the combination finesse in spades. This has mathematically a 3 to 1 chance (actually about 74 per cent) of succeeding and there is the further point that West has already turned up with ace and king of clubs. To be sure of sufficient entries to dummy, South should lead a low heart on the second round. No matter if this loses to a doubleton queen: there will still be sufficient entries for two finesses in spades, and in all probability the declarer will lose just one spade, one heart and one club.

Dealer, South   Neither side vulnerable

       ♠ K 8 5 3
       ♡ 10 7 4
       ◇ K 10 8 2
       ♣ 6 3

♣ J led

       ♠ A 7 4
       ♡ A K 3
       ◇ Q 9
       ♣ A K Q 5 2

South	West	North	East
2♣(1)	pass	2◇	pass
2NT	pass	3NT(2)	pass
pass	pass		

Final contract—3NT

(1) South proposes to follow the sequence 2♣ – 2◇ – 2NT, not forcing in his system.

(2) North could have responded three clubs, asking for four-card suits, but he appears to have ample support for game in notrump and any inquiry is likely to be of more help to the defenders than to his own side.

The early play

West leads the jack of clubs and East plays the 4. Content with the club attack, South ducks. West continues with the 8 of clubs, East discards a low diamond, and South wins. How should South plan the play?

First look

After the disappointment in clubs declarer has seven top tricks and at least one can readily be established in diamonds. He needs to find one more.

Problem No. 29

It may be possible to establish an extra trick in spades, but there is no hurry for that and declarer may think that the obvious beginning is to attack diamonds by leading the queen from hand. But that may not be so clever!

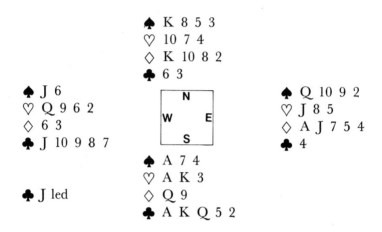

♠ K 8 5 3
♡ 10 7 4
◇ K 10 8 2
♣ 6 3

♠ J 6
♡ Q 9 6 2
◇ 6 3
♣ J 10 9 8 7

♠ Q 10 9 2
♡ J 8 5
◇ A J 7 5 4
♣ 4

♠ A 7 4
♡ A K 3
◇ Q 9
♣ A K Q 5 2

♣ J led

Playing in 3NT, South wins the second round of clubs and leads the queen of diamonds. East plays low and declarer suddenly finds that he has no reliable way of arriving at a ninth trick.

Leading the queen of diamonds may also fail if West holds the ace of diamonds and East the jack. West may duck on the first two rounds, forcing South to a guess.

Thanks to the high spot cards in diamonds South can make sure of the contract by leading the 9 at trick three and letting it run if not covered. If the 9 holds, South can follow with the queen, establishing a second trick. If the 9 loses to the jack, then South wins the return and overtakes the queen of diamonds with the king, again ensuring two diamond tricks.

Dealer, South   Neither side vulnerable

> ♠ J 5
> ♡ 8 6 2
> ◇ K J 10 9 4
> ♣ A 10 6

♡ J led

> ♠ A Q 9 3
> ♡ A K Q
> ◇ A Q 2
> ♣ Q J 5

South	West	North	East
2♣	pass	3◇	pass
3NT(1)	pass	4NT(2)	pass
5◇	pass	6NT	pass
pass	pass		

Final contract—6NT

(1) South's first duty is to show that he has a balanced hand on which he would have rebid 2NT over a negative response of two diamonds. He can trust his partner to advance if not minimum.

(2) Not conventional, when bid by the weaker hand after a two club opening.

The early play

West leads the jack of hearts, on which his partner plays the 4. How should South plan the play?

First look

South has ten certain tricks by way of five diamonds, three hearts and two aces. There are finesse positions in both black suits and also the possibility of dropping the 10 of spades in three rounds.

Problem No. 30

A successful finesse in either black suit will win the contract, as declarer can immediately turn to the other suit. On the other hand, a losing finesse places the contract in jeopardy.

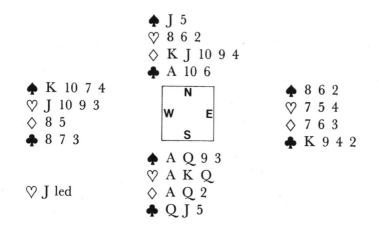

```
                    ♠ J 5
                    ♡ 8 6 2
                    ◇ K J 10 9 4
                    ♣ A 10 6
  ♠ K 10 7 4          N           ♠ 8 6 2
  ♡ J 10 9 3                       ♡ 7 5 4
  ◇ 8 5          W        E        ◇ 7 6 3
  ♣ 8 7 3                          ♣ K 9 4 2
                     S
                    ♠ A Q 9 3
                    ♡ A K Q
  ♡ J led           ◇ A Q 2
                    ♣ Q J 5
```

South is in 6NT and West leads the jack of hearts. If South takes a losing finesse in clubs he will have to take the spade finesse later. The disadvantage of finessing in spades at once is that West may switch to a club, and declarer will then have to decide whether to take the club finesse or play for the 10 of spades to drop in three rounds.

There are three chances—the two finesses and the drop of the spade 10. The way to take advantage of all three chances is to lead a low spade from hand at trick two. If West has the king and plays it, there will be three tricks in spades. If the jack of spades wins, South can turn to clubs. If the jack of spades loses to East's king, the best that East can do is return a spade. South can then try for the drop of the 10 of spades before taking a club finesse.

Dealer, West   Neither side vulnerable

♠ J 10 8 4
♡ 10 9 7 5
◇ A 10 4
♣ 6 5

♡ 8 led

♠ K Q 9 7 3 2
♡ A J
◇ K 7
♣ K 8 3

South	West	North	East
—	1 ♣	pass	1 ♡
2 ♠ (1)	pass	3 ♠	pass
4 ♠	pass	pass	pass

Final contract—Four Spades

(1) If you play weak jump overcalls you must double. You are better placed here if your system is to play strong jump overcalls at equal vulnerability.

The early play
West leads the 8 of hearts, East plays the queen and South the ace. How should South continue?

First look
West is sure to hold the ace of clubs, so South must attempt to guard against the loss of a heart, a spade and two clubs.

Problem No. 31

To the declarer, the hand seemed to present a routine elimination play: ruff out the diamonds, then play a trump, hoping that West will have no more hearts and will be compelled to open up the clubs.

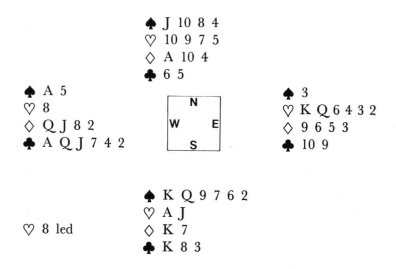

♠ J 10 8 4
♡ 10 9 7 5
♢ A 10 4
♣ 6 5

♠ A 5
♡ 8
♢ Q J 8 2
♣ A Q J 7 4 2

♠ 3
♡ K Q 6 4 3 2
♢ 9 6 5 3
♣ 10 9

♠ K Q 9 7 6 2
♡ A J
♢ K 7
♣ K 8 3

♡ 8 led

South played in four spades after West had opened one club and East had responded one heart. West led the 8 of hearts to the queen and ace.

Aiming to leave West on play with the ace of spades, South played three rounds of diamonds, ruffing the third round, then led a low spade from hand. West was not so foolish as to duck; he went up with the ace and exited with a trump, leaving the declarer with two club losers.

When East played low on the third round of diamonds South had a guaranteed play for the contract. Instead of ruffing, he must discard his jack of hearts. Now the 10 9 7 in dummy are equals against East's king, and South can organize two discards via a ruffing finesse. It makes no difference whether West has a singleton heart or a doubleton.

This line is also likely to win if West's diamonds are Q x x instead of Q J x x. To avoid the sequence described above, West must be smart enough to jettison his queen of diamonds on the first or second round.

Dealer, South Both sides vulnerable

```
              ♠ 8 6 4 3
              ♡ K
              ◇ A K 5
              ♣ 10 7 4 3 2
♠ Q led
              ♠ A 5 2
              ♡ A 10 9 4
              ◇ 10 8 3
              ♣ A K 5
```

South	*West*	*North*	*East*
1 NT	pass	2 ♣ (1)	pass
2 ♡	pass	3 NT	pass
pass	pass		

Final contract—3NT

(1) Although players habitually use Stayman on this type of 5–4–3–1 hand, there is little to be said for it. Even if you do reach a spade contract the trumps will be weak. Meanwhile, your singleton is a king and, like the clubs, may be useful in notrump. Facing a 15–17 notrump, a raise to 3NT is the more sensible action.

The early play

West leads the queen of spades and East overtakes with the king. East returns the 7 and South wins with the ace. How should South plan the play?

First look

Declarer must hope to make the contract by way of one spade, two hearts, two diamonds and four clubs.

Problem No. 32

South can count nine tricks on the assumption that the clubs will break reasonably well, but there may be an entry problem.

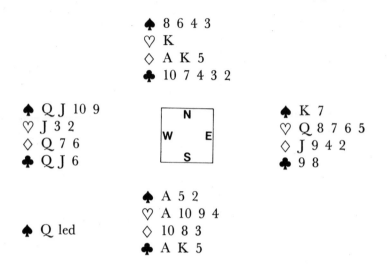

♠ 8 6 4 3
♡ K
◇ A K 5
♣ 10 7 4 3 2

♠ Q J 10 9
♡ J 3 2
◇ Q 7 6
♣ Q J 6

♠ K 7
♡ Q 8 7 6 5
◇ J 9 4 2
♣ 9 8

♠ A 5 2
♡ A 10 9 4
◇ 10 8 3
♣ A K 5

♠ Q led

West leads the queen of spades against 3NT. East overtakes and returns the 7, which South wins.

It may seem natural to play off ace, king and another club, but if he does this the declarer will be cut off from the ace of hearts. West will cash two spades and exit with a heart. South will make the rest of the clubs but will lose a diamond at the finish.

It would not help to play off the king of hearts before taking three rounds of clubs, because then West would exit with a diamond after cashing his spades.

The way to overcome a block of this kind is to duck an early round of clubs. A safe sequence is to cross to the king of hearts, cash the ace of clubs and lead a low club. West makes a club and two spades, but the entry position is now fluid. Say that West exits with a diamond: South wins in dummy, crosses to the king of clubs and cashes the ace of hearts. Then he returns to dummy with a diamond to make the long clubs.

Dealer, West Neither side vulnerable

```
                    ♠ 9 7 3
                    ♡ K J
                    ◇ 8 5 4 2
                    ♣ J 10 6 3
◇ 3 led
                    ♠ A K Q 8 6 2
                    ♡ A 10
                    ◇ A 9 6
                    ♣ A K
```

South	West	North	East
—	pass	pass	1 ◇
2 ◇	pass	3 ♣	pass
3 ♠	pass	4 ♠	pass
4 NT (1)	pass	5 ♣	pass
5 ◇	pass	5 ♡	pass
6 ♠ (2)	pass	pass	pass

Final contract—Six Spades

(1) South knows, of course, that his partner will be unable to show an ace in response to the Blackwood 4NT. His idea is to make another slam try over five clubs, thus making it clear that he is interested in a slam despite the absence of aces in the North hand.

(2) South's plan appears to have worked well. With the king of hearts opposite, there should be a good play for the slam.

The early play

West leads the 3 of diamonds. Even though East's opening bid may have been psychic, he is likely to hold five diamonds, so South must capture the first trick. On the second round of spades East discards a low club. How should South plan the play?

First look

There is unfortunate duplication in hearts and prospects seem poor when the queen of clubs does not fall in two rounds.

Problem No. 33

At the risk of going two down instead of one down, South can give himself a chance for the contract.

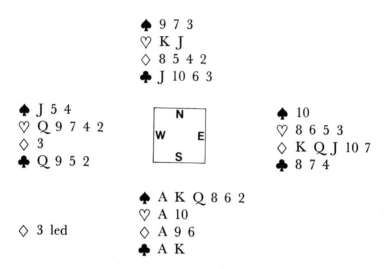

♠ 9 7 3
♡ K J
◇ 8 5 4 2
♣ J 10 6 3

♠ J 5 4
♡ Q 9 7 4 2
◇ 3
♣ Q 9 5 2

N
W E
S

♠ 10
♡ 8 6 5 3
◇ K Q J 10 7
♣ 8 7 4

◇ 3 led

♠ A K Q 8 6 2
♡ A 10
◇ A 9 6
♣ A K

South plays in six spades after East has opened with a psychic one diamond in third position.

South wins the diamond lead and draws three rounds of trumps, East discarding one club and one diamond. The ace and king of clubs fail to bring down the queen. Now South may seem to have no way of avoiding the loss of two diamond tricks, but an attractive combination of entry-finesse and jettison play enables him to make use of dummy's J 10 of clubs.

After three rounds of spades and two rounds of clubs South leads the 10 of hearts and successfully finesses the jack. Then he leads the jack of clubs from the table, discarding the ace of hearts. West wins but must give dummy the lead, allowing South to discard one diamond on the king of hearts and one on the 10 of clubs.

5. Developing Tricks in a Side Suit

In perhaps the majority of suit contracts the declarer will attempt to establish low-card tricks in a side suit. The problems in this section are concerned with communication, trump control, and probabilities.

When declarer seeks to establish a trick by ruffing he must take care not to put high cards unnecessarily at risk.

A Q J 7 4 2

8

Suppose that you intend to develop this suit by means of a ruffing finesse against the king. It may be a mistake to play the ace and then run the queen. If the trump holding and entries permit, begin by ruffing a low card. This will save tricks when either defender holds a doubleton king. It is the same with A J 10 9 5 opposite a singleton queen: with sufficient trumps, lead the queen to the ace and ruff a low card on the next round. Again, you save a trick when either defender holds K x.

Players are often uncertain about the best way to develop four winners with this combination:

A Q 8 5 3 2

6

If you play the ace and later ruff two low cards, you will arrive at four tricks whenever the king falls in two or three rounds. In general, however, you do better to finesse the queen. As compared with the other method, this will gain when West holds K x x x, will lose when East holds K x, a less likely division.

When developing a side suit, the declarer will often use the trump suit for entry. It is not always clear whether to test the side suit before the trumps or the other way round.

```
                    ♠ K 10 5
                    ♡ A Q 6 5 4
                    ◇ J 4 2
                    ♣ 7 3

♠ 8 6 4 3          ┌─────────┐          ♠ 7
♡ 9 8 3            │    N    │          ♡ J 10 7
◇ A K 9            │ W     E │          ◇ Q 10 7 3
♣ 10 8 4           │    S    │          ♣ K Q J 9 2
                   └─────────┘

                    ♠ A Q J 9 2
                    ♡ K 2
◇ K led             ◇ 8 6 5
                    ♣ A 6 5
```

West led the king of diamonds against four spades. After three rounds of diamonds East switched to the king of clubs.

Judging that a 4–2 break in hearts was more likely than 4–1 in spades, South began by ruffing the third round of hearts. When he found the trumps 4–1 he could not get back to dummy to enjoy the hearts. Here it would have been correct to take two rounds of trumps first. Finding that spades are not breaking, declarer must play for hearts to be 3–3.

Nevertheless, it is generally better play to test the side suit first.

```
                    ♠ 6 4
                    ♡ 5
                    ◇ A J 9 5
                    ♣ A K 8 6 4 2

♠ Q led

                    ♠ A 8 3
                    ♡ 9 7 6 4 2
                    ◇ K Q 10 3
                    ♣ 7
```

A spade is led against five diamonds. Here it is right to begin with ace, king and another club. If clubs are 3–3, South can cope with diamonds 4–1; if clubs are 4–2 he must play for the trumps to be 3–2.

Dealer, South Both sides vulnerable

        ♠ Q 8 3
        ♡ Q
        ♢ 8 5 4 2
        ♣ K Q 10 8 3

♡ K led

        ♠ A K J 9 7 4
        ♡ J 2
        ♢ A Q 6
        ♣ J 5

South	West	North	East
1 ♠	pass	2 ♣	pass
2 ♠ (1)	pass	3 ♠	pass
4 ♠	pass	pass	pass

Final contract—Four Spades

(1) South is strong for the simple rebid, at any rate by Acol standards, but he was playing the Blue Club style in which a response at the two level is forcing to 2NT. If responses at the two level are kept up to a fair standard, there are many advantages in this method.

The early play
West leads the king of hearts and follows with the ace. How should South plan the play?

First look
South has a losing heart and a losing club, so the contract seems to depend on not losing two tricks in diamonds.

Problem No. 34

The declarer may easily lose his way on this contract before he has adjusted his sights.

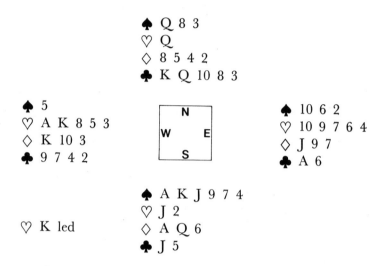

♠ Q 8 3
♡ Q
◇ 8 5 4 2
♣ K Q 10 8 3

♠ 5
♡ A K 8 5 3
◇ K 10 3
♣ 9 7 4 2

♠ 10 6 2
♡ 10 9 7 6 4
◇ J 9 7
♣ A 6

♠ A K J 9 7 4
♡ J 2
◇ A Q 6
♣ J 5

♡ K led

South plays in four spades and West begins with king and ace of hearts. Suppose that South ruffs in dummy and attempts to force out the ace of clubs. East wins the second round and leads the 9 of diamonds. The finesse of the queen loses and West returns a diamond to the ace. South plays two rounds of trumps, finishing in dummy, but the trumps don't break and East ruffs the next club, so declarer must lose a second diamond at the finish.

What has gone wrong? Quite simple—South should not ruff the second lead in dummy, but should discard a diamond. Now West cannot profitably attack diamonds, nor can he shorten dummy's trumps. Whatever happens next, South can draw two high trumps from hand, then play on clubs, with the queen of spades as an entry after the clubs have been established.

Dealer, South   Neither side vulnerable

♠ A K Q 6 5
♡ A 10 3
♢ 6 4
♣ A 8 3

♢ Q led

♠ 7 3
♡ K Q J 5
♢ A K 8 2
♣ Q 5 2

South	West	North	East
1 ♡	pass	2 ♠	pass
2NT (1)	pass	3 ♡	pass
4 ♢ (2)	pass	5 ♣	pass
5 ♢	pass	6 ♡	pass
pass	pass		

Final contract—Six Hearts

(1) South's first duty is to show that his hand is comparatively balanced. After rebidding 2NT he can always "come again."

(2) This is a cue-bid, indicating that South is better than minimum and has a control in diamonds.

The early play

West leads the queen of diamonds, East plays the 3, and South wins with the ace. How should he plan the play?

First look

There are ten tricks in top cards. It should be safe to ruff one diamond at least, and there is the obvious possibility of at least one extra trick in spades. However, entries may be a problem, especially if the trumps are 4–2.

Problem No. 35

The play looks simple at first: take one diamond ruff, draw trumps, then develop a fourth trick in spades. This adds up to twelve tricks by way of two diamonds, a ruff, four top trumps, four spades (assuming a 4–2 break), and one club. Yet this sequence may easily fail, as the following diagram shows:

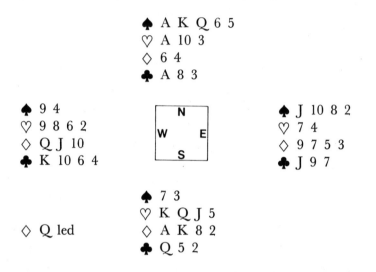

♠ A K Q 6 5
♡ A 10 3
◇ 6 4
♣ A 8 3

♠ 9 4
♡ 9 8 6 2
◇ Q J 10
♣ K 10 6 4

♠ J 10 8 2
♡ 7 4
◇ 9 7 5 3
♣ J 9 7

◇ Q led

♠ 7 3
♡ K Q J 5
◇ A K 8 2
♣ Q 5 2

South is in six hearts and West leads the queen of diamonds. Suppose that South wins, ruffs the third round of diamonds with the 10 of hearts, and draws trumps. He plays off three top spades but cannot develop a long spade without giving East the lead. When he wins the fourth round of spades East is able to cash the 9 of diamonds.

The solution is to give up a spade trick early on, before the defenders can make a trick in any other suit. Win the first diamond and duck a spade immediately. Whatever the return, South can win it and then switch back to diamonds. He takes the diamond ruff, draws trumps, and makes four tricks in spades. This line succeeds unless diamonds are 6–1 or one of the major suits is 5–1.

Dealer, South   Neither side vulnerable

♠ 4 2
♥ K 9 5 3
♦ —
♣ A J 10 9 6 4 3

♦ Q led

♠ A K 7 5 3
♥ A Q J 4
♦ A 8 6
♣ 5

South	West	North	East
1 ♠	pass	2 ♣	pass
2 ♥	pass	4 ♥ (1)	pass
6 ♥ (2)	pass	pass	pass

Final contract—Six Hearts

(1) A jump to four diamonds would indicate the void and the heart support, but North is a trifle under strength for that sequence. Four diamonds would be right if he held better trumps or an additional value such as the queen of spades.

(2) South does not mind much where his partner's strength lies, so he bids the slam directly.

The early play

West leads the queen of diamonds. How should South plan the play?

First look

South must decide how to play to the first trick and whether to set up his own hand or the dummy.

Problem No. 36

If the trumps are 3–2 South has good chances whether he plays on clubs or spades. If he intends to play on clubs, probably the best line is to take the first trick with the ace of diamonds and play a club to the ace. To finesse the club 9 on the first round would be a losing play if East held a singleton queen or king.

To play on the spades is better because then South may be able to stand a 4–1 break in trumps. Suppose that the cards lie like this:

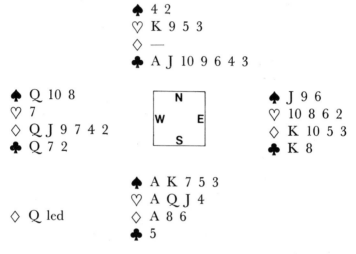

```
                    ♠ 4 2
                    ♡ K 9 5 3
                    ◇ —
                    ♣ A J 10 9 6 4 3

  ♠ Q 10 8           N             ♠ J 9 6
  ♡ 7          W          E        ♡ 10 8 6 2
  ◇ Q J 9 7 4 2        S           ◇ K 10 5 3
  ♣ Q 7 2                          ♣ K 8

                    ♠ A K 7 5 3
                    ♡ A Q J 4
  ◇ Q led           ◇ A 8 6
                    ♣ 5
```

South is in six hearts and West leads the queen of diamonds. It is not important whether South ruffs or wins with the ace. Say that he ruffs, plays a spade to the ace, ruffs another diamond, and returns to the spade king. Now he ruffs a spade with the king of hearts and plays off his three top trumps. As the cards lie, he loses only a trump trick.

Had the spades been 4–2, South would have needed to find the hearts 3–2. His line fails only if spades are 4–2 and hearts 4–1. Playing on the clubs will almost certainly fail whenever trumps are 4–1, and in most cases when the clubs are 4–1.

Dealer, South Both sides vulnerable

♠ A Q J 7 5
♡ 7 5 3
◇ 4
♣ K Q 9 3

♡ K led

♠ 6
♡ A 8 4 2
◇ K 5
♣ A J 10 7 5 2

South	West	North	East
1 ♣	pass	1 ♠	pass
2 ♣	pass	3 ◇ (1)	pass
3 ♡	pass	4 ♣	pass
4 ♠ (2)	pass	6 ♣ (3)	pass
pass	pass		

Final contract—Six Clubs

(1) As a change of suit to two diamonds would be forcing in his system, North's jump to three diamonds confirms clubs and promises first or second round control of diamonds.

(2) As clubs are the agreed suit, South can make a cue-bid in spades without fear of being misunderstood.

(3) It would be foolish to bid a Blackwood 4NT, because if partner has only one ace the response will already take the partnership beyond five clubs. As the bidding has gone, North can be sure his partner has two aces.

The early play

West leads the king of hearts, East plays the 6 and South wins with the ace. How should South plan the play?

First look

The hands do not fit too well, with K x of diamonds opposite a singleton. Declarer has two problems—how to play the spades and how to discard when the suit has been established.

Problem No. 37

The play calls just for intelligent planning. Declarer can count on six club tricks, ace of hearts and a diamond ruff. He will therefore need to develop four tricks in spades. He must play for this type of distribution:

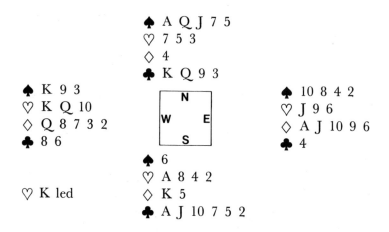

♠ A Q J 7 5
♡ 7 5 3
◇ 4
♣ K Q 9 3

♠ K 9 3
♡ K Q 10
◇ Q 8 7 3 2
♣ 8 6

♠ 10 8 4 2
♡ J 9 6
◇ A J 10 9 6
♣ 4

♡ K led

♠ 6
♡ A 8 4 2
◇ K 5
♣ A J 10 7 5 2

Playing in six spades, South wins the heart lead and should at once finesse the queen of spades, as he intends to play West for K x x. Then he ruffs a low spade, draws trumps, finishing in dummy, and is able to cash three spade winners when the king falls under the ace. He must be careful to discard hearts, not diamonds. Then he can give up a diamond and make his twelfth trick with a diamond ruff.

To take the ruffing finesse in spades—leading a spade to the ace and returning the queen—would succeed only against one particular distribution. At best, South would be able to organize two diamond discards, one on the jack of spades, one on the fifth spade. Then he would ruff dummy's diamond and play ace and another heart, with some end-play possibilities.

Problem No. 38

Dealer, South   E–W vulnerable

```
              ♠ 8 4
              ♡ 10 7 6 4 2
              ◇ A 8 5
              ♣ 9 6 3
♡ K led
              ♠ A K 9 6 5
              ♡ —
              ◇ 10 4
              ♣ A K Q 10 7 5
```

South	West	North	East
2♣(1)	pass	2◇	pass
3♣	pass	3♡	pass
3♠	pass	4♣(2)	pass
5♣(3)	pass	pass	pass

Final contract—Five Clubs

(1) The hand is not strong in high cards for a conventional two club opening, but the bid may deter the opposition.

(2) The hand plays easily in 3NT, but North's support for clubs, ace of diamonds, and doubleton spade, suggest a possible slam.

(3) South might have bid four spades at this point.

The early play

West leads the king of hearts and East plays the 5. South ruffs and lays down the ace of spades, to which all follow. How should South continue?

First look

If spades are 3–3 and clubs 2–2 South may sail home with thirteen tricks. But suppose spades are 4–2 and clubs 3–1: there will be a danger then of losing two spades (or a spade and overruff) and a diamond.

Problem No. 38

No problem will arise if the spades split 3–3 and the play will be simple enough if East holds four spades. (West may ruff the third round with the jack of clubs, but South will be able later to ruff the fourth spade with the 9 of clubs.) The dangerous distribution is where East has a doubleton spade and good enough trumps to overruff the dummy twice.

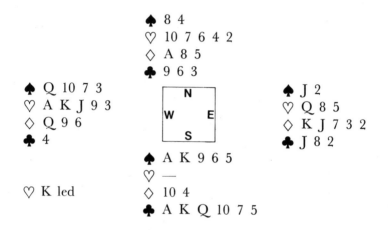

```
                    ♠ 8 4
                    ♡ 10 7 6 4 2
                    ◇ A 8 5
                    ♣ 9 6 3
♠ Q 10 7 3                          ♠ J 2
♡ A K J 9 3        N                ♡ Q 8 5
◇ Q 9 6         W     E             ◇ K J 7 3 2
♣ 4                   S             ♣ J 8 2
                    ♠ A K 9 6 5
                    ♡ —
♡ K led             ◇ 10 4
                    ♣ A K Q 10 7 5
```

South plays in five clubs and is happy to receive a heart rather than a diamond lead. He must, of course, develop the spades before drawing trumps. Suppose he begins with ace, king and another spade. If he ruffs, he is overruffed and will then not be able to escape the loss of another spade and a diamond.

A double loser-on-loser play wins the contract. When West follows to the third round of spades South must discard a diamond from dummy. Another heart from West is as good as anything. South ruffs and plays a fourth spade, again discarding a diamond from the table. West may play a third heart, but South is in command. He leads a diamond to the (now single) ace, returns to hand with a trump, and ruffs his diamond loser. Then he draws trumps and his last spade is a master.

Dealer, North   Neither side vulnerable

♠ A K J
♡ A 9 7 6 4 2
◇ K Q 9
♣ 5

♠ 10 led

♠ Q 3
♡ K 5
◇ A J 8 5 2
♣ Q 7 4 2

South	West	North	East
—	—	1 ♡	pass
2 ◇	pass	2 ♠	pass
2NT	pass	3 ◇	pass
3 ♡	pass	3 ♠ (1)	pass
4 ◇ (2)	pass	6 ◇	pass
pass	pass		

Final contract—Six Diamonds

(1) A good choice because it gives partner several options: to sign off in 3NT, rebid the diamonds, cue-bid in clubs, or settle for four hearts.

(2) The club guard is not sufficiently robust for 3NT. As the heart holding is ideal for a slam in diamonds, South confirms that he has a fair diamond suit.

The early play

West leads the 10 of spades, the king is played from dummy, and East drops the 6. How should South plan the play?

First look

South can count on five diamonds, three spades and two hearts. One club ruff will not be enough for the slam, and to play for two club ruffs is awkward. It looks, therefore, as though declarer must aim to establish the hearts.

Problem No. 39

The simple line is to draw trumps and trust the hearts will be 3–2. It is slightly better to test the hearts after two rounds of trumps, because the same player may hold a singleton heart and only two diamonds. That is unlikely, and the contract will usually fail when the hearts are not breaking.

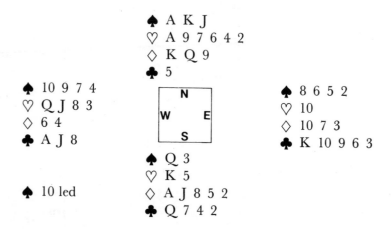

```
                    ♠ A K J
                    ♡ A 9 7 6 4 2
                    ◇ K Q 9
                    ♣ 5
♠ 10 9 7 4                                  ♠ 8 6 5 2
♡ Q J 8 3           N                       ♡ 10
◇ 6 4          W         E                  ◇ 10 7 3
♣ A J 8                 S                   ♣ K 10 9 6 3

                    ♠ Q 3
                    ♡ K 5
♠ 10 led            ◇ A J 8 5 2
                    ♣ Q 7 4 2
```

South is in six diamonds and West leads a spade, won by the king. If declarer draws trumps he will be short of entries to set up the hearts, and if he plays king and ace of hearts early on he will run into a ruff.

Declarer can protect himself against a 4–1 break in hearts by a stratagem that is commonly overlooked. The best sequence is: king of spades, heart to the king, discard the 5 of hearts on the third spade. A low heart is led from dummy and the break is revealed when East discards. South ruffs, crosses to the king of diamonds and ruffs another low heart. When the diamonds break, the dummy hand is high except for the losing club.

There is a slight risk of a spade ruff in this line of play, but a doubleton spade in the East hand will not be immediately fatal, and hearts are more likely to be 4–1 than spades 6–2.

Dealer, South   Both sides vulnerable

♠ 5
♡ J 9 7 4 3
◇ A 9 8
♣ A 7 5 4

◇ K led

♠ A Q J 8 7 4
♡ A
◇ 7
♣ K J 8 6 3

South	West	North	East
1♠	pass	1NT(1)	pass
3♣(2)	pass	4◇(3)	pass
6♣	pass	pass	pass

Final contract—Six Clubs

(1) This hand was played in a match between two top teams. It is a matter of style whether North should respond 1NT or two hearts.

(2) Partners who respond 1NT to one spade sometimes hold a singleton spade, so it is sensible to mention the clubs. The jump to three clubs need not be played as game-forcing: either player can pass later if the bidding develops in a disappointing way.

(3) The jump shows diamond control and good club support.

The early play

West leads the king of diamonds to dummy's ace. All follow to the ace of clubs. How should South continue?

First look

If trumps are 2–2, straightforward play will win the contract unless the spades are very badly distributed. South must think about the possibility of trumps being 3–1 and spades 4–2.

Problem No. 40

This hand was misplayed at both tables in the match. Both declarers, after winning the diamond lead, drew two rounds of trumps with the ace and king. The lie of the cards soon showed that this was a mistake:

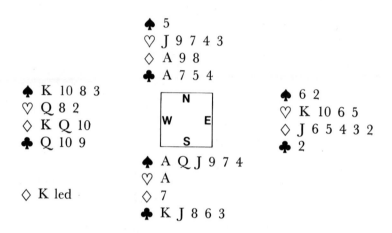

```
                    ♠ 5
                    ♡ J 9 7 4 3
                    ◇ A 9 8
                    ♣ A 7 5 4
♠ K 10 8 3                              ♠ 6 2
♡ Q 8 2          ┌──────────┐          ♡ K 10 6 5
◇ K Q 10         │    N     │          ◇ J 6 5 4 3 2
♣ Q 10 9         │ W      E │          ♣ 2
                 │    S     │
                 └──────────┘
                    ♠ A Q J 9 7 4
                    ♡ A
◇ K led             ◇ 7
                    ♣ K J 8 6 3
```

Playing in six clubs, South wins the diamond lead and plays ace and king of clubs. He cashes ace of spades and ruffs a low spade, returns to the ace of hearts and leads the queen of spades, on which West plays the 10.

South is now in a dilemma. If he lets the queen run he may lose to the king. If he ruffs, and finds the spades 4–2, he will again have to give up a trick to the king of spades, as dummy will be out of trumps.

South has much better control if he does not draw a second trump. After ace of clubs he plays a spade to the ace and ruffs a spade, returns to ace of hearts and ruffs another spade. As the cards lie, this is not overruffed and South can set up the suit by ruffing another spade later.

And if trumps are 2–2 and East is able to overruff the third round of spades? No matter, because East will not be able to play a third round of trumps.

It is the old principle: attend to the side suit before drawing trumps.

6. Trump Management and Control

Most hands played in a suit contract belong to one of two main types. Either the declarer has trump control, or thinks he has, and accordingly he aims to draw the opponents' trumps and make tricks in side suits; or he neglects the trump suit and plays a crossruff game after cashing top winners in the side suits. Sometimes it is not entirely clear to which group the hand belongs.

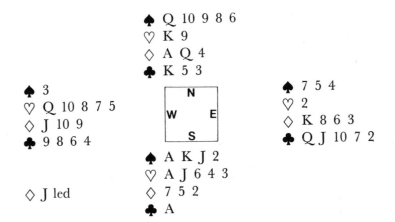

♠ Q 10 9 8 6
♡ K 9
◇ A Q 4
♣ K 5 3

♠ 3
♡ Q 10 8 7 5
◇ J 10 9
♣ 9 8 6 4

♠ 7 5 4
♡ 2
◇ K 8 6 3
♣ Q J 10 7 2

◇ J led

♠ A K J 2
♡ A J 6 4 3
◇ 7 5 2
♣ A

South plays in six spades and West leads the jack of diamonds. Most players would plan to discard a diamond from hand on the king of clubs, then draw trumps and play on hearts. The bad distribution in hearts kills the contract. If you look at it again you will see that it is not exactly a crossruff type, but that declarer can make almost sure of the contract by taking two ruffs in his own hand. The play goes: ace of diamonds, club to ace, spade to 9, king of clubs (pitching a diamond), club ruff, give up a diamond; no problem now in ruffing the third round of diamonds and drawing trumps. In a masters pairs event half the field went down in six spades.

This is another hand that calls for a second look:

```
              ♠ A K 3
              ♡ 9 8
              ◊ 9 7 6 5 2
              ♣ A K 6

◊ Q led
              ♠ J 7 6 4
              ♡ A K Q 10 3
              ◊ —
              ♣ J 8 5 2
```

South is in four hearts and West leads the queen of diamonds. Do you see a fairly safe way to ten tricks? Just play the deal as a reverse dummy: ruff the diamond lead, enter dummy in turn with the winners in the black suits, ruffing altogether five diamonds. Barring accidents, you will have made nine tricks by now, and dummy's 9 8 of hearts, being equals against the jack, can be relied on to supply the tenth.

There are many ways of preventing the defenders from gaining trump control. Two methods are illustrated in the following deal:

```
              ♠ 9 5
              ♡ J 7 4
              ◊ A 10 6 3
              ♣ A 8 4 2

♡ K led
              ♠ A K J 10 3
              ♡ 8
              ◊ K Q 5 2
              ♣ K J 7
```

South plays in four spades after the defenders have bid and supported hearts. West leads king and ace of hearts and South ruffs the second round. To enter dummy with either of the minor suit aces involves a slight loss of control, and South's best play now is the 10 of spades from hand. The opponents win with the queen and lead a third heart. Now South does not ruff, but discards a diamond. Then dummy's 9 of spades is protection against a fourth round of hearts. Playing in this fashion, South retains control against Q x x x of spades in the West hand.

It is especially important not to lose trump control when you have a long suit in dummy which you may expect to run. Here South employs the same kind of stratagem as in the previous example:

♠ Q 7 4
♡ 8 2
◇ 10 6
♣ A Q J 7 4 3

◇ K led

♠ A 8 6 2
♡ A K Q 7 3
◇ J
♣ K 8 2

South is in four hearts and the defenders begin with two rounds of diamonds. South might decline to ruff, throwing a spade, but the simplest line is to ruff and lead a low heart. Say that East wins and leads a spade: South can take the ace, draw trumps, and run the clubs. This safety play will always win unless the trumps are 5–1.

You may think that South would make the contract if he ruffed the second diamond and played off ace, king and queen of hearts. If hearts are 3–3 he will make twelve tricks, but if they are 4–2 he will not be well placed. Obviously he cannot play a fourth round of trumps to drive out the winner; and if he turns to clubs, the defenders will presumably have the wit to break communications by holding up their master trump until the third round. After ruffing the third club they will exit with a diamond. South will then need to find the spades well placed.

It is sometimes important not to give the opponents a chance to cash a master trump at a time when they can draw "two for one." The next deal is more tricky than it may seem.

South is in four hearts and West leads the 9 of trumps. It does not look far wrong to win with the king, cross to the ace of spades, and run the jack of clubs. If the finesse loses, you plan to discard a spade from dummy on the third round of

                    ♠ A 8 3
                    ♡ 10 6 5 2
                    ◇ A J 5 4
                    ♣ J 5

♡ 9 led

                    ♠ K 7 6 4
                    ♡ A K 4 3
                    ◇ 8 2
                    ♣ A Q 10

---

clubs. This way, you expect to lose one trump, one diamond and one club. South played in this fashion and lost the contract, though the distribution was quite normal:

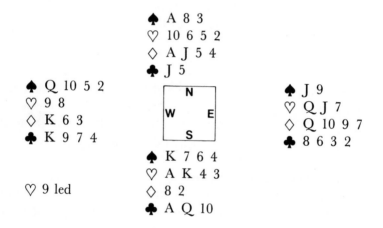

                    ♠ A 8 3
                    ♡ 10 6 5 2
                    ◇ A J 5 4
                    ♣ J 5

♠ Q 10 5 2   ♠ J 9
♡ 9 8   ♡ Q J 7
◇ K 6 3   ◇ Q 10 9 7
♣ K 9 7 4   ♣ 8 6 3 2

                    ♠ K 7 6 4
                    ♡ A K 4 3
♡ 9 led   ◇ 8 2
                    ♣ A Q 10

Playing in four hearts, South captured the heart lead, crossed to the ace of spades, and ran the jack of clubs to West's king. West led a second heart. South won, discarded a spade on the third round of clubs, and followed with king of spades and a spade ruff. East did not make the mistake of overruffing. Instead, he won the next trick with the 9 of diamonds and then led the queen of hearts, drawing two for one. Now South had no parking place for his fourth spade.

Here East was the danger hand, in the sense that East was likely to hold the three trumps. The simplest line is to duck a diamond at trick two, extracting East's entry before he can cash a master trump.

Dealer, South   E–W vulnerable

```
              ♠ 7
              ♡ 10 3
              ◇ Q 10 8 5
              ♣ Q 7 6 5 3 2
♡ K led
              ♠ A K Q J 9 4
              ♡ 7
              ◇ K J 9 3
              ♣ K 8
```

South	West	North	East
South	*West*	*North*	*East*
2♠(1)	pass	2NT	pass
3♠	pass	4♠(2)	pass
pass	pass		

Final contract—Four Spades

(1) South is playing the Acol system in which two bids are forcing for one round. The hand is lacking in quality for a two bid, but the show of strength may be a good tactical move, especially at this vulnerability.

(2) Borderline, but one of the objects of a two bid is to extract a response from a partner who would pass a bid of one. North may reasonably hope that his two queens will pull some weight.

The early play

West opens the king of hearts and continues with the queen, which South ruffs. How should South plan the play?

First look

Both dummy's queens are useful, so it looks as though the contract should be made for the loss of three aces.

Problem No. 41

Despite the possible danger of a diamond ruff, South cannot afford to draw trumps immediately. If he does this he will be open to defeat whenever the trumps are 4–2.

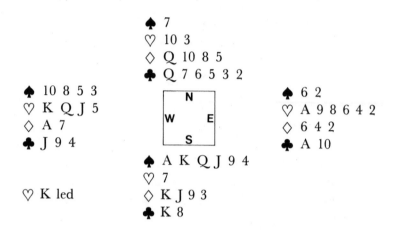

♠ 7
♡ 10 3
◇ Q 10 8 5
♣ Q 7 6 5 3 2

♠ 10 8 5 3
♡ K Q J 5
◇ A 7
♣ J 9 4

♠ 6 2
♡ A 9 8 6 4 2
◇ 6 4 2
♣ A 10

♡ K led

♠ A K Q J 9 4
♡ 7
◇ K J 9 3
♣ K 8

Playing in four spades, South ruffs the second round of hearts. Now suppose that he draws four rounds of trumps: there will still be two aces to force out, and when his trumps are exhausted South will lose the last two tricks—the ace of clubs and a heart.

The singleton trump in dummy is capable of performing a useful function. At trick three South should establish a club trick by leading the 8 to the queen and ace. Now if East continues hearts, dummy can ruff and South can regain the lead with the king of clubs. Then he can draw trumps and will still have a trump left after he has forced out the ace of diamonds.

As the cards lie, South also succeeds if he plays the king of clubs at trick three instead of low to the queen, but the other play is slightly better.

Problem No. 42

Dealer, South   Neither side vulnerable

> ♠ 10 6 2
> ♡ K J 8 6 5 3
> ◇ Q 4
> ♣ A 8

◇ 6 led

> ♠ A 8 7 5 4 3
> ♡ A 10 2
> ◇ J 3
> ♣ K 6

South	West	North	East
1♠	pass	2♡	pass
2♠	pass	3♠	pass
pass(1)	pass	pass	pass

Final contract—Three Spades

(1) Playing in a pairs event, South does not press for what must surely be a doubtful game.

The early play

West leads the 6 of diamonds, East wins with the ace and returns the 5 to West's king. West exits with the 5 of clubs. How should South plan the play?

First look

South has lost two tricks already and must seek to avoid the loss of two spades and a heart.

Problem No. 42

In four spades the obvious line would be to eliminate the clubs, then lead ace another spade, hoping for a 2–2 split. In three spades the play is more subtle.

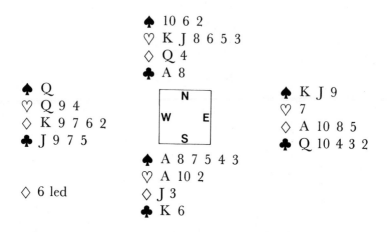

West leads a diamond against three spades. The defenders take two diamond tricks and switch to a club.

If the spades are 3–1 South will be in danger of losing five tricks. His best line after eliminating the second club is to lead a low spade from hand. This gains when either defender holds a high singleton. In the present case West wins with the queen and must then either open up the hearts or concede a ruff-and-discard. Either way, South is spared the necessity of making a blind guess in hearts.

An experienced defender in the East position, appreciating the reason for the lead of a low trump, might overtake the queen of spades with the king and return the 9. If this happens, South must not be deceived into thinking that East holds K 9 alone: it is perfectly safe to play low again from hand, because if West is able to win with the jack he will be on lead as before.

Dealer, West   Both sides vulnerable

```
                    ♠ 7 6 5 2
                    ♡ K 10
                    ◊ J 7 4 3
                    ♣ K 7 4
♠ K led
                    ♠ J 3
                    ♡ Q J 9 8 5
                    ◊ A K
                    ♣ A Q 6 3
```

South	West	North	East
—	1 ♠	pass	pass
dble	pass	2 ◊	pass
2 ♡	2 ♠	3 ♡	pass
pass(1)	pass		

Final contract—Three Hearts

(1) Not far short of four hearts, but South has bid quite strongly and must not penalize his partner for giving him what may have been just a competitive raise.

The early play

West begins with three top spades. East discards a diamond on the third round and South ruffs. How should he continue?

First look

South appears to have nine fairly solid tricks—four hearts and five top cards in the minor suits. However, it may not be easy to draw trumps and cash the club winners.

Problem No. 43

It may not matter if East has four trumps, but four trumps in the hand that holds the long spades will certainly create a problem.

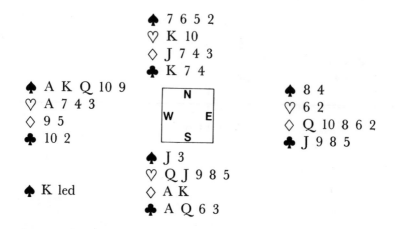

♠ 7 6 5 2
♡ K 10
♢ J 7 4 3
♣ K 7 4

♠ A K Q 10 9
♡ A 7 4 3
♢ 9 5
♣ 10 2

♠ 8 4
♡ 6 2
♢ Q 10 8 6 2
♣ J 9 8 5

♠ K led

♠ J 3
♡ Q J 9 8 5
♢ A K
♣ A Q 6 3

South plays in three hearts after West has opened one spade. West begins with three top spades and South must ruff. If he now leads trumps, West will win the second round and force again in spades. This will leave West with more trumps than declarer and a long spade to make as well.

Often the solution on a hand like this is to play off three rounds of clubs before touching trumps, preparing to ruff the fourth round if necessary. But here West will ruff the third round and play ace and another trump, leaving South with a club loser.

Now try a different line: ace and king of diamonds, ace of clubs, king of clubs, and duck a club! If the defenders draw trumps, South will make the queen of clubs in due course, and if they do anything else South will be able to ruff the queen of clubs with a high trump.

The play of ducking the third club is difficult to recognize in this setting unless South concentrates on the number of winners required: he needs either five trump tricks and two clubs or four trumps and three clubs.

Dealer, West   Both sides vulnerable

♠ A 10 6 2
♥ J 9 5 4
♦ A 9
♣ A Q J

♦ K led

♠ 7 5 4
♥ 10 7 6 2
♦ J 4
♣ K 7 5 3

South	West	North	East
—	1 ◇	dble	pass
1 ♡	pass	2 ♡ (1)	pass
pass	pass	pass	

Final contract—Two Hearts

(1) The raise to two hearts may seem obvious, as indeed it does to me, but many players will not raise a forced response unless they hold "the earth." This leads to an unbalanced situation in which the responder to a take-out double feels impelled to jump on a moderate holding such as five to the king and a side king. It is much better for the doubler to raise when he has a fit and about a king above a minimum. Then the responder is not called upon to give a jump response unless he has fair values.

The early play
West leads the king of diamonds, the ace is played from dummy, and East drops the 3. How should South plan the play?

First look
After the diamond lead South is confronted by the prospect of six losers—three in trumps, two in spades and one in diamonds. There is more than one possible way of saving a trick, and South's problem is to find the best way.

Problem No. 44

Against moderate opposition it is sometimes possible to persuade a defender into an unwise cover in the trump suit. South may think of leading the jack of hearts from dummy; a poor player in the East position might cover with Q x x or K x x and cause a crash of high cards.

There are also slight possibilities in elimination play. Suppose that West holds a doubleton K J or K Q in spades. South plays a trump at trick two, the defenders win, cash a diamond, and exit in spades or clubs. After three rounds of clubs the declarer plays another trump and the player who wins this trick may be awkwardly placed, forced to lead a diamond.

However, if trumps are 3–2 and clubs 3–3 there is a better line of play.

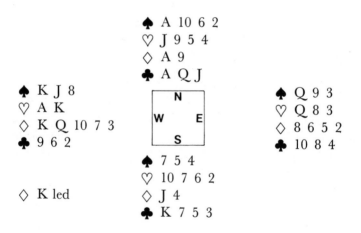

$\spadesuit$ A 10 6 2
$\heartsuit$ J 9 5 4
$\diamondsuit$ A 9
$\clubsuit$ A Q J

$\spadesuit$ K J 8
$\heartsuit$ A K
$\diamondsuit$ K Q 10 7 3
$\clubsuit$ 9 6 2

$\spadesuit$ Q 9 3
$\heartsuit$ Q 8 3
$\diamondsuit$ 8 6 5 2
$\clubsuit$ 10 8 4

$\diamondsuit$ K led

$\spadesuit$ 7 5 4
$\heartsuit$ 10 7 6 2
$\diamondsuit$ J 4
$\clubsuit$ K 7 5 3

Playing in two hearts, South wins the diamond lead in dummy and plays three rounds of clubs, overtaking with the king. When all follow, he leads a fourth club, discarding a diamond from dummy. Whichever opponent ruffs, it is at the cost of a trump trick.

Even if the third round of clubs is ruffed, South will not necessarily lose an extra trick. It is worth noting, too, that since the opponents, with nine diamonds and 20 points between them, have not competed, the distribution is probably balanced.

Dealer, West   Both sides vulnerable

```
              ♠ 10 8 7
              ♡ 3 2
              ◇ K 7 4 2
              ♣ J 9 8 2
♣ 10 led
              ♠ K 5
              ♡ K Q 10 9 7 6
              ◇ A Q 5
              ♣ 6 3
```

South	*West*	*North*	*East*
—	1♠	pass	2♣
2♡(1)	dble	pass	pass
pass			

Final contract—Two Hearts doubled

(1) This overcall is about to receive the axe, but it could hardly be criticized.

The early play

West leads the 10 of clubs, which is covered by the jack and queen. East cashes a high club, to which all follow, then switches to a spade. West makes the jack and ace of spades and continues with the queen. East follows suit and South ruffs. How should he continue?

First look

South has lost four tricks already and must expect to lose two trump tricks as well, in view of West's penalty double. At this point, remember, every undertrick will cost an additional 300!

Problem No. 45

The full hand was:

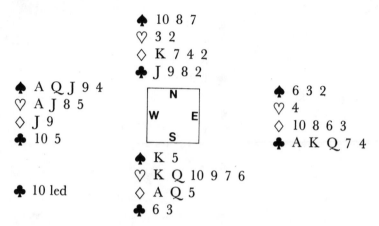

```
                  ♠ 10 8 7
                  ♡ 3 2
                  ◇ K 7 4 2
                  ♣ J 9 8 2
♠ A Q J 9 4          N              ♠ 6 3 2
♡ A J 8 5       W        E          ♡ 4
◇ J 9                               ◇ 10 8 6 3
♣ 10 5               S              ♣ A K Q 7 4
                  ♠ K 5
♣ 10 led          ♡ K Q 10 9 7 6
                  ◇ A Q 5
                  ♣ 6 3
```

West led a club against two hearts doubled. The best defence
is to return a spade at trick two, but East cashed a second club.
After two clubs and three rounds of spades the position was:

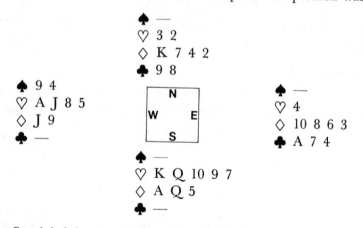

```
                  ♠ —
                  ♡ 3 2
                  ◇ K 7 4 2
                  ♣ 9 8
♠ 9 4                N              ♠ —
♡ A J 8 5       W        E          ♡ 4
◇ J 9                               ◇ 10 8 6 3
♣ —                  S              ♣ A 7 4
                  ♠ —
                  ♡ K Q 10 9 7
                  ◇ A Q 5
                  ♣ —
```

South led the queen of hearts and West ducked. When he won
the next heart West forced declarer with a spade and so made
his fourth heart, for a penalty of 500.

South failed to realize that dummy's 3 2 of hearts afforded
protection against a forcing game. He saves a trick if in the
diagram position he leads the 9 or 10 of hearts, letting West win
with the jack. Then dummy can take care of a further spade
from West.

Dealer, North   Neither side vulnerable

♠ K 10 5
♡ 9 3
◇ A Q J 2
♣ Q J 8 4

♠ 9 led

♠ —
♡ A Q J 10 6 4
◇ K 9 5 3
♣ 10 6 2

South	West	North	East
—	—	1◇	1♠
2♡(1)	3♠	pass	pass
4♡(2)	pass	pass	pass

Final contract—Four Hearts

(1) Some players would bid two spades at this point, to express the diamond support and spade control, but it is far better to show where the values lie and, if necessary, indicate the controls later.

(2) Four diamonds, in the competitive situation, would not be forcing, and the hearts are reasonably self-supporting.

The early play

South covers the 9 of spades with dummy's 10, East plays the jack, and South ruffs. How should he plan the play?

First look

On the surface there are only three losers, two clubs and possibly one heart, but the club trick is not immediate and there may be problems of control.

Problem No. 46

It may seem natural to cross to dummy at trick two and take the heart finesse. But see where that leads, against quite normal distribution:

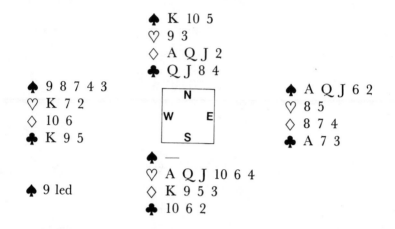

```
                    ♠ K 10 5
                    ♡ 9 3
                    ◇ A Q J 2
                    ♣ Q J 8 4
  ♠ 9 8 7 4 3       ┌─────────┐      ♠ A Q J 6 2
  ♡ K 7 2           │    N    │      ♡ 8 5
  ◇ 10 6            │ W     E │      ◇ 8 7 4
  ♣ K 9 5           │    S    │      ♣ A 7 3
                    └─────────┘
  ♠ 9 led           ♠ —
                    ♡ A Q J 10 6 4
                    ◇ K 9 5 3
                    ♣ 10 6 2
```

Playing in four hearts, South ruffs the spade lead, crosses to dummy with a diamond and runs the 9 of hearts, losing to West's king. West leads another spade and South must ruff again. After drawing trumps he has only one heart left and will not have time to establish a trick in clubs. He will make five tricks in hearts and four in diamonds, but that will be all.

It is better, on such hands, to tackle the side suit at once. South leads a club at trick two. The best defence is for West to go up with the king of clubs and lead another spade, forcing South to ruff. The ace of clubs is forced out and East plays a third spade, reducing the declarer to A Q J of hearts. But now South leads the queen of hearts and dummy's nine of hearts is protection against a fourth round of spades.

By playing clubs early on, South obviously runs the risk of a ruff in clubs or possibly in diamonds. But he still has the heart finesse in reserve and, as we have seen, if the heart finesse is wrong he cannot make the contract anyway, except by leading clubs early on and trusting the suit to be divided 3–3.

Dealer, South   Neither side vulnerable

♠ 8 4 2
♡ 9 4 3
♢ 7 6 5 2
♣ 8 6 3

♣ J led

♠ A K Q J 10
♡ A 7 5 2
♢ K Q
♣ A Q

South	West	North	East
2♣	pass	2♢	pass
2♠	pass	2NT	pass
3♡	pass	3♠	pass
4♠(1)	pass	pass	pass

Final contract—Four Spades

(1) To bid 3NT now is not attractive, because North will be declarer and there may be a lead through the A Q of clubs. There was, however, something to be said for a rebid of 3NT over North's two diamonds.

The early play

West leads the jack of clubs, East plays the 4, and South wins with the queen. How should South plan the play?

First look

The opening lead has solved one of declarer's problems. He needs now to avoid the loss of one diamond and three hearts.

Problem No. 47

It is usually right to attend to side suits before drawing trumps. Here, for example, if South begins by playing spades he will eventually lose three tricks in hearts.

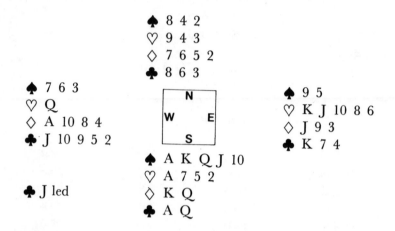

♠ 8 4 2
♡ 9 4 3
◇ 7 6 5 2
♣ 8 6 3

♠ 7 6 3
♡ Q
◇ A 10 8 4
♣ J 10 9 5 2

♠ 9 5
♡ K J 10 8 6
◇ J 9 3
♣ K 7 4

♣ J led

♠ A K Q J 10
♡ A 7 5 2
◇ K Q
♣ A Q

After winning the first trick with the queen of clubs, the declarer correctly led a heart at trick two. Even one round of trumps might be a mistake, for if a defender with four hearts held three trumps he might be able to extract dummy's trumps before the fourth heart could be ruffed.

At the table, South made a common error by beginning with a *low* heart. As a rule this will not cost, but on this occasion East overtook his partner's queen and fired back the jack. West ruffed and South had still to lose a heart and the ace of diamonds. There was nothing to gain by beginning with a low heart. South should play ace of hearts first. As the cards lie, the fourth round can be ruffed with dummy's eight of spades.

The correspondent who sent me this deal added a touching postscript: "I was North. Am I right in thinking that a player with no card higher than a 9 can ask for a new deal?"

You can ask, but try it at my club!

Dealer, East   Neither side vulnerable

```
                    ♠  —
                    ♡  J 7 4 3
                    ◇  A K Q J
                    ♣  A J 10 6 4
    ♠ K led
                    ♠  A 8 5 2
                    ♡  9 8 5
                    ◇  7 3
                    ♣  K 9 5 2
```

South	*West*	*North*	*East*
—	—	—	pass
pass	1♠	dble	1NT
2♣(1)	pass	5♣(2)	pass
pass	pass		

Final contract—Five Clubs

(1) Some players would double 1NT, but when partner has made a take-out double it is seldom wrong to name one's best suit.

(2) This seems a fair gamble and North does not want to assist opponents to find the best lead.

The early play

West's lead of the king of spades is ruffed in dummy. Declarer lays down the ace of clubs and all follow. How should he continue?

First look

Having escaped a heart lead, South has an obvious opportunity to discard two hearts on dummy's diamonds; but meanwhile he must consider how to play the trump suit.

Problem No. 48

Did you decide to play for the drop in trumps or to play East for Q x x? Neither play would be right!

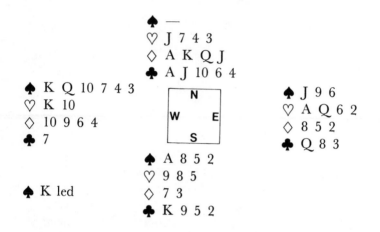

```
                    ♠ —
                    ♡ J 7 4 3
                    ◊ A K Q J
                    ♣ A J 10 6 4
♠ K Q 10 7 4 3              N           ♠ J 9 6
♡ K 10              W           E       ♡ A Q 6 2
◊ 10 9 6 4                 S            ◊ 8 5 2
♣ 7                                    ♣ Q 8 3
                    ♠ A 8 5 2
                    ♡ 9 8 5
♠ K led             ◊ 7 3
                    ♣ K 9 5 2
```

In a match between France and Sweden the declarer in five clubs ruffed the spade lead and played ace and king of clubs, failing to drop the queen. He thought that East's 1NT quite possibly concealed spade support and that there was no good reason to risk an immediate finesse.

South then took four rounds of diamonds, discarding two hearts. East did not make the mistake of ruffing the fourth round with his master trump. Instead, he went up with the ace of hearts on the first round of the suit and then drew two trumps for one. This left the declarer a trick short.

It was wrong to draw a second round of trumps when there was a danger that a defender would come in to draw a third round. So long as diamonds are 4–3, the contract is safe. After one round of trumps South plays off the diamonds. Suppose, at worst, that trumps are 2–2 and West ruffs the fourth diamond. The defenders can make their heart trick, but South can draw the last trump and make the rest of the tricks on a crossruff.

Dealer, North   Both sides vulnerable

♠ —
♡ A Q J
◇ 8 7 6 5
♣ A 9 6 5 3 2

◇ 10 led

♠ K J 6 4
♡ K 9 3
◇ K Q 3 2
♣ K 7

South	West	North	East
—	—	1♣	pass
1◇	pass	2◇	pass
3NT	pass	4♣(1)	pass
4◇	pass	5◇	pass
pass	pass		

Final contract—Five Diamonds

(1) This might be wrong, but North is naturally reluctant to play in notrump when holding a void in an unbid suit. Partner is likely to hold the king of hearts, so there should be a play for game in one of the minor suits.

The early play

West leads the 10 of diamonds, East plays the 4 and South wins with the king. How should South plan the play?

First look

It looks as though the only possible losers are in the trump suit, but a 4–1 break in either minor suit could prove awkward.

Problem No. 49

It is tempting, perhaps, to ruff a spade at trick two, but see what that leads to:

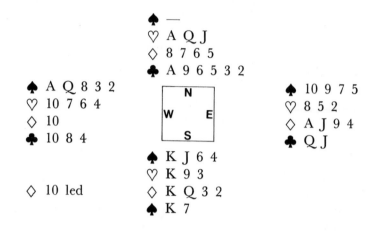

```
                    ♠ —
                    ♡ A Q J
                    ◇ 8 7 6 5
                    ♣ A 9 6 5 3 2
  ♠ A Q 8 3 2        N           ♠ 10 9 7 5
  ♡ 10 7 6 4     W       E       ♡ 8 5 2
  ◇ 10              S           ◇ A J 9 4
  ♣ 10 8 4                       ♣ Q J
                    ♠ K J 6 4
                    ♡ K 9 3
  ◇ 10 led          ◇ K Q 3 2
                    ♠ K 7
```

As the bidding had shown that the North hand was unbalanced, West led his singleton trump against five diamonds. East played low and South won. Attracted by the void in spades, South ruffed a spade and led a low diamond from dummy. East promptly went up with the ace and returned the jack, extracting dummy's last trump. When East later made the 9 of diamonds he led a spade and West collected two spade tricks, for a penalty of 200.

When he ruffed the spade at trick two, South was playing the enemy's game. As his trumps are fragile, the last thing he should do is weaken them by ruffing. He should cross to dummy with a heart and lead a trump from the dummy. The best that East can do is win with the ace and lead a spade, forcing dummy to ruff. South must now play three rounds of clubs, ruffing the third round, cross to the queen of hearts, and lead the established clubs. When East ruffs he is allowed to hold the trick. It is a difficult exercise in trump management.

Dealer, South   Neither side vulnerable

<pre>
                      ♠ Q 9
                      ♡ 8 5 4
                      ◇ J 6 5 4 2
                      ♣ A Q 2
   ♡ 2 led
                      ♠ A K J 5 4
                      ♡ J
                      ◇ A 7
                      ♣ K J 10 8 6
</pre>

South	West	North	East
1♣	pass	1◇	1♡
1♠	2♡	3♣	pass
3♠	pass	4♡(1)	pass
4♠	dble	pass	pass
pass(2)			

Final contract—Four Spades

(1) This is quite an interesting and imaginative bid. The North hand is limited by his previous three clubs, so the meaning of four hearts now is that he has support for both spades and clubs and is not sure in which suit to play.

(2) South realizes that the spade situation may not be secure, but it is certain that five clubs will be doubled as well, and there again a bad break in spades will be damaging.

The early play

West leads the 2 of hearts to his partner's king and East returns a heart. How should South plan the play?

First look

If trumps were 4–2 there would be eleven tricks on top, but West's double of four spades is a clear warning that they may be 5–1. Thus trump control is going to be a problem.

Problem No. 50

When West, who has simply raised his partner's overcall, doubles four spades, he is marked with five trumps. Even with that knowledge, South must play very accurately to land the contract.

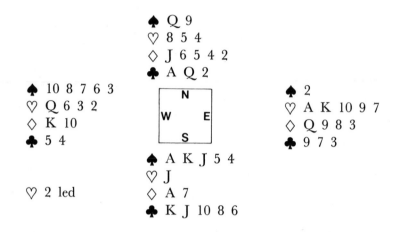

```
                    ♠ Q 9
                    ♡ 8 5 4
                    ◇ J 6 5 4 2
                    ♣ A Q 2
  ♠ 10 8 7 6 3           N              ♠ 2
  ♡ Q 6 3 2      W              E       ♡ A K 10 9 7
  ◇ K 10                                ◇ Q 9 8 3
  ♣ 5 4                 S              ♣ 9 7 3
                    ♠ A K J 5 4
                    ♡ J
  ♡ 2 led           ◇ A 7
                    ♣ K J 10 8 6
```

South is in four spades doubled and the defenders begin with a heart to the king and a heart back. On general principles (though it is not essential here) South should discard a diamond on the second trick. This is a certain loser and by discarding the diamond now he restricts communications between the defending hands. A third heart is led and now he must ruff.

South has lost two tricks already and if he tries to draw trumps he will inevitably lose two more, as West will have the long trump and another heart to lead. The best line is to cash the queen of spades and then play three rounds of clubs, allowing West to ruff if he wants to.

If West ruffs the third club he can do no damage, as dummy's 9 of spades will be protection against another round of hearts. If the third club is not ruffed, South simply leads a fourth club.

7. Inter-relationship

You cannot, as they say, pour a quart into a pint pot. The significance, in bridge terms, of this homely illustration is that the declarer must always bear in mind (a) that each opponent started with thirteen cards, and (b) that the high-card strength of each defender must fall within certain limits, determined by his bidding or failure to bid. The problems in this section depend on assumption, discovery and hypothesis.

By way of introduction, here are two deals where declarer succeeds in dropping a doubleton queen, apparently against the odds.

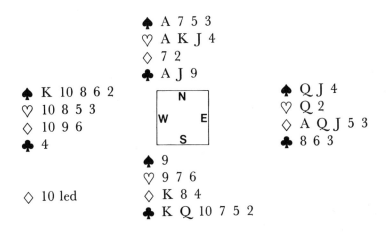

South is in six clubs and West leads the 10 of diamonds. East wins with the ace and returns the queen.

The contract appears to depend on the heart finesse, but the declarer should defer this play until the last possible moment. After winning with the king of diamonds, he plays a spade to the ace and ruffs a spade, takes his diamond ruff, and draws trumps. Then he plays a heart to the ace and ruffs another spade. He reaches this end position:

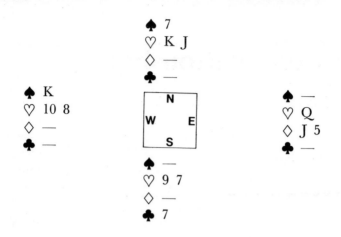

South leads the last club and West throws a heart, dummy a spade, and East a diamond. On the 7 of hearts West plays the 10 and declarer must go up with the king because he can be fairly certain that West's last card is a spade.

On this next deal the declarer proceeds on a similar voyage of discovery:

```
              ♠ K Q 5
              ♡ Q 10 7 2
              ◇ K 9 6 4 2
              ♣ 3
♠ J 7 4          N          ♠ 10 8 6 3 2
♡ A 8 4      W       E      ♡ 9 5 3
◇ Q J 10 8 5     S          ◇ 3
♣ Q 5                       ♣ 9 6 4 2
              ♠ A 9
◇ Q led       ♡ K J 6
              ◇ A 7
              ♣ A K J 10 8 7
```

West leads the ◇Q against 6NT. South wins, forces out the ♡A, and wins the next diamond in dummy. After cashing his winners he is down to A K J 10 of clubs and needs all the tricks.

Declarer knows that West started with three spades, three hearts and five diamonds, so he can have two clubs at most. East (who has not discarded a club) is known to have four clubs left. It is no use finessing the jack of clubs, so declarer must play for the drop of the queen and happily succeeds.

Dealer, North   Both sides vulnerable

```
              ♠ K Q 5
              ♡ K 7 4 2
              ◇ J 4 3
              ♣ K 7 4
♠ 9 led
              ♠ 6 4 2
              ♡ —
              ◇ A Q 10 8 5 2
              ♣ A Q J 3
```

South	West	North	East
—	—	pass	pass
1 ◇	pass	2NT(1)	pass
3 ♣	pass	3 ◇	pass
5 ◇ (2)	pass	pass	pass

Final contract—Five Diamonds

(1) After a pass, especially, a natural 2NT is preferable to a scientific one heart. Some players, when they have passed on 12 points, feel impelled to bid 3NT on the next round, as though the fact that they had passed made the hand stronger.

(2) South could bid four hearts at this point, indicating the void, but it is unlikely that he will find partner with the right cards for a slam. Better, therefore, to bid the game without giving away information.

The early play

West leads the 9 of spades, East covers the queen with the ace and returns the jack to dummy's king. How should South plan the play?

First look

If East had held five spades he would surely have ducked the first trick to retain communication. It looks very much, therefore, as though declarer cannot afford to lose a trump trick.

Problem No. 51

There is a small trap here: you may think that the critical move is to lead the jack of diamonds from dummy, so that if East turns up with K 9 7 6 you will be able to re-enter dummy with the king of clubs and pick up the trumps without loss. That is a valid point, but a more practical consideration is whether to attempt to drop a singleton king of trumps. A discovery play may supply the answer.

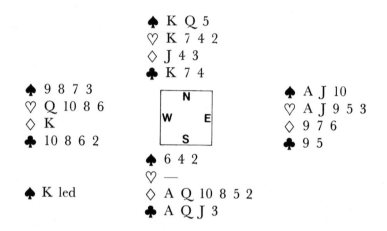

South plays in five diamonds after opening third in hand. The 9 of spades is covered by the queen and ace and the jack of spades is returned to dummy's king.

East has already shown A J 10 of spades. If he has the ace of hearts as well, he can hardly have the king of diamonds, as he passed originally. South should put this to the test by leading the king of hearts from dummy at trick three. If East plays the ace, then it becomes mandatory to play off the ace of diamonds on the first round.

A good player in East's position might read the declarer for a void in hearts and play low without a tremor when the king was led. This defence would not avail here, because South would simply discard his losing spade.

Dealer, West   Both sides vulnerable

♠ K 8 5
♡ Q 10 3
◇ A 8 5 4
♣ K 6 2

♡ 4 led

♠ A Q J 9 6 2
♡ 7 2
◇ 10 7 6
♣ A 10

South	West	North	East
—	pass	pass(1)	3♡
3♠	pass	4♠(2)	pass
pass	pass		

Final contract—Four Spades

(1) Even those hardy folk who play a weak notrump throughout at rubber bridge might hesitate to open this unproductive assortment.

(2) North has a fairly close decision whether to bid 3NT or four spades. As he has enough to think that four spades might be lay-down, he decides not to risk a possible calamity in notrump.

The early play

West leads the 4 of hearts and East plays three top hearts, South ruffing high on the third round. West, meanwhile, discards a low diamond and a low club. Trumps fall in two rounds. How should South plan the play from this point?

First look

South has lost two tricks already and needs to avoid the loss of two diamonds.

Problem No. 52

The diamond combination of A x x x opposite 10 x x offers various possibilities for elimination play. The best play will depend on how the diamonds are divided. West's discards—one club and one diamond—suggest 5–5 in these suits. It is therefore right to play on the assumption that East has a singleton rather than a doubleton diamond. (If East were 2–7–2–2, South could squeeze West in the minor suits.)

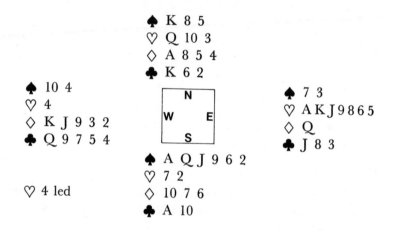

Playing in four spades, South ruffs the third round of hearts high and draws trumps in two rounds. Then he plays three rounds of clubs, eliminating this suit and at the same time obtaining a count of the East hand.

As expected, East follows to three rounds of clubs. He can now be counted for a singleton diamond. South must hope that the singleton is a high card, as indeed is likely. He plays a low diamond from each hand. Whoever takes this trick will be left on play, with no good lead.

It may seem that East would do better to lead the queen of diamonds at trick three, to avoid the end-play. In this case declarer can eliminate the clubs, play two rounds of trumps, finishing in dummy, and exit with the queen of hearts. When East covers (not having played three rounds early on), South discards a diamond and East is left on play.

Dealer, East   N–S vulnerable

♠ K 6 5 3
♡ 9 4
◇ K 8 3
♣ 8 7 4 2

♡ A led

♠ A 10
♡ J 3
◇ A J 10 9 5 4
♣ A K 6

South	West	North	East
—	—	—	3 ♡
dble	pass	3 ♠	pass
4 ◇	pass	5 ◇ (1)	pass
pass	pass		

Final contract—Five Diamonds

(1) South has followed a strong sequence and North is entitled to think that his two kings will pull enough weight for game to be a fair proposition.

The early play

West leads the ace of hearts and follows with the 2 to his partner's queen. East switches to the 10 of clubs. How should South plan the play?

First look

South has two problems: he must pick up the trump suit without loss and must somehow develop an extra trick in black suits.

Problem No. 53

East is marked with seven hearts, so it may seem logical to play him for short diamonds. But if you play East for a singleton diamond, how will you avoid losing a club?

You must start from the other end, taking the black suits first. The only chance of an extra trick here lies in a squeeze, and for this to work West must hold exclusive control of both spades and clubs. He must, in fact, hold at least five spades and four clubs. (If spades were 4–3 you could establish a threat card by ruffing the third round, but because of the entry situation the lone spade on the table would not help you to develop a squeeze.)

So you must assume—because this is your only hope of avoiding the loss of a club—that West holds nine cards in the black suits. Since he has already shown two hearts he cannot (following the assumption you have been forced to make) hold three diamonds.

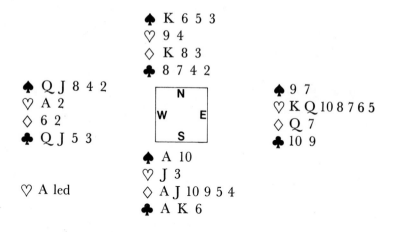

<pre>
                    ♠ K 6 5 3
                    ♡ 9 4
                    ◇ K 8 3
                    ♣ 8 7 4 2
♠ Q J 8 4 2   N   ♠ 9 7
♡ A 2   W   E   ♡ K Q 10 8 7 6 5
◇ 6 2   ◇ Q 7
♣ Q J 5 3   S   ♣ 10 9
                    ♠ A 10
                    ♡ J 3
♡ A led   ◇ A J 10 9 5 4
                    ♣ A K 6
</pre>

South plays in five diamonds after East has opened three hearts. The defenders begin with two rounds of hearts, followed by a club switch. Having decided that the contract will be impossible if West holds three diamonds, South plays a diamond to the king and a diamond back, on which the queen appears. Then he plays off all the diamonds and West is forced to unguard one of the black suits.

Dealer, North   Neither side vulnerable

```
              ♠ J 8 3
              ♡ K J 7 4
              ◇ J
              ♣ K 8 7 6 2
♡ 10 led

              ♠ A Q 9 7 6 5 2
              ♡ —
              ◇ A K Q 10
              ♣ Q 3
```

South	West	North	East
—	—	pass	pass
2♠(1)	pass	3♣	pass
3◇	pass	4♠(2)	pass
6♠(3)	pass	pass	pass

Final contract—Six Spades

(1) South is playing the Acol system, in which two bids are forcing for one round.

(2) Opposite a two bid, J x x is very fair support, and North takes the opportunity to express this.

(3) South does not try for seven, as he does not expect his partner to hold K x x of spades and A K of clubs. With those values North would have marked time with three spades over three diamonds.

The early play

West leads the 10 of hearts, the jack is covered by the queen, and South ruffs. How should South plan the play?

First look

The ace of clubs is a certain loser, so the contract will depend on not losing a trick in spades.

Problem No. 54

With J 8 3 opposite A Q 9 7 6 5 2 the safety play is to lead the jack on the first round, enabling the declarer to pick up K 10 x on his right. However, that is not the point of the present problem.

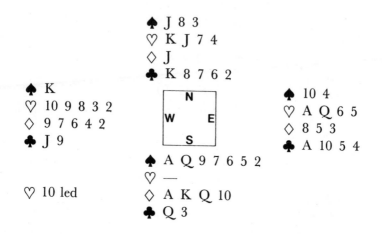

```
                        ♠ J 8 3
                        ♡ K J 7 4
                        ◇ J
                        ♣ K 8 7 6 2
    ♠ K                 ┌─────────────┐          ♠ 10 4
    ♡ 10 9 8 3 2        │      N      │          ♡ A Q 6 5
    ◇ 9 7 6 4 2         │  W       E  │          ◇ 8 5 3
    ♣ J 9               │      S      │          ♣ A 10 5 4
                        └─────────────┘
                        ♠ A Q 9 7 6 5 2
                        ♡ —
    ♡ 10 led            ◇ A K Q 10
                        ♣ Q 3
```

South opens two spades after two passes and finishes in four spades. West leads the 10 of hearts, the jack is covered by the queen, and South ruffs.

Declarer could enter dummy with the jack of diamonds to lead the jack of spades, but it should occur to him that East, who passed originally, is marked by the opening lead with A Q of hearts. If East has the ace of clubs as well, then he can scarcely hold a guarded king of spades.

South explores this possibility at trick two by leading a club to the king and ace. After that, he has no hesitation in dropping the singleton king of spades.

Dealer, South   Neither side vulnerable

```
              ♠ 9 3 2
              ♡ K 8 6 2
              ◇ A Q 6
              ♣ K 5 4
♣ 9 led
              ♠ A Q
              ♡ A 10 9 7 4
              ◇ 8 3
              ♣ A Q J 2
```

South	West	North	East
1♡	pass	3♡	pass
4♣	pass	4◇	pass
4♡(1)	pass	5♣(2)	pass
6♡	pass	pass	pass

Final contract—Six Hearts

(1) South has made a slam try and is not entitled, on his own, to carry the bidding beyond game level.

(2) North raised only to three hearts on the first round (not forcing in his system), because of the balanced distribution. However, his hand is good for slam purposes and he therefore decides to show the control in clubs.

The early play
West's lead of the 9 of clubs runs to the declarer's queen, East playing low. On a low heart to the king West plays the queen. How should South continue?

First look
After the queen of hearts has appeared on the first round there are finesse positions in three suits. South must look for a line of play that will improve on the separate chances.

Problem No. 55

The best chance of avoiding a loser in the trump suit, considered on its own, is to finesse on the next round rather than play for the drop. (This is in line with the theory of restricted choice, described in my book, *The Expert Game*.) South finessed at the table and lost the contract, for the full hand was:

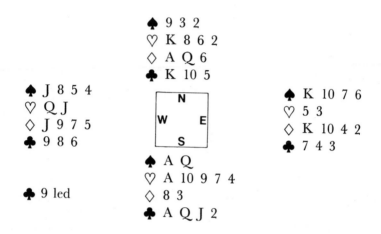

♠ 9 3 2
♡ K 8 6 2
♢ A Q 6
♣ K 10 5

♠ J 8 5 4
♡ Q J
♢ J 9 7 5
♣ 9 8 6

♠ K 10 7 6
♡ 5 3
♢ K 10 4 2
♣ 7 4 3

♠ A Q
♡ A 10 9 7 4
♢ 8 3
♣ A Q J 2

♣ 9 led

Playing in four hearts, South won the club lead, played a heart to the king and finessed on the way back. After that, he could not avoid the loss of a diamond as well.

It was not exactly a mistake to finesse in the trump suit, but it was a mistake to put this matter to the test early on.

The significant point is that since the spade finesse must be taken at some stage, it should be taken first. If it wins, South will know how to play the trumps, so at trick two he plays a heart to the king and finesses the queen of spades. When it holds, he lays down the ace of hearts. If the jack falls, he can finesse in diamonds for an overtrick. If the jack does not fall, he continues with ace of spades, a club to the king, and a spade ruff. The remaining clubs are played off and sooner or later East (if he began with J x x of hearts) will be thrown in and forced to lead a diamond or a spade.

The point to remember is that when a finesse position contains no tactical possibilities it should be taken early. South may be able to avoid the diamond finesse, but once he has begun with a heart to the king he must always take the spade finesse.

Dealer, West   Both sides vulnerable

♠ —
♡ A Q 10 9 7 4
♢ A 9 6 2
♣ Q J 9

♠ K led

♠ 9 7 4
♡ J 8
♢ K J 8 7 3
♣ A 10 3

South	West	North	East
—	1♠	2♡	2♠
3♢(1)	3♠	4♠	pass
5♣(2)	pass	6♢	pass
pass	pass		

Final contract—Six Diamonds

(1) South could support the vulnerable overcall, but he has in mind the possibility of attracting a good lead should opponents buy the contract in spades.

(2) If partner is void in spades South is not averse to the idea of a slam in diamonds.

The early play

West leads the king of spades. South ruffs in dummy and leads ace of diamonds, to which all follow, and another diamond, on which East plays the 10. How should South plan the play?

First look

If the heart finesse is right (and West holds no more than three hearts) the contract cannot fail. On the other hand, if the heart finesse is wrong it will be essential to locate the queen of diamonds. Thus the critical decision is whether to finesse in diamonds or play for the drop.

Problem No. 56

South is unlikely to fail in this contract if the heart finesse is right. He should therefore assume that it is wrong and that he must make the winning play in diamonds.

However, the question of how to play the diamonds is a problem in two parts: not just whether 3–1 or 2–2 is more likely, but whether a correct view of this suit will necessarily bring home the contract.

To find the diamonds 2–2 will clearly leave the declarer with no worries. But suppose the distribution is something like this:

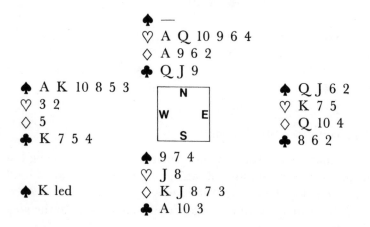

♠ —
♡ A Q 10 9 6 4
◇ A 9 6 2
♣ Q J 9

♠ A K 10 8 5 3
♡ 3 2
◇ 5
♣ K 7 5 4

♠ Q J 6 2
♡ K 7 5
◇ Q 10 4
♣ 8 6 2

♠ 9 7 4
♡ J 8
◇ K J 8 7 3
♣ A 10 3

♠ K led

South ruffs the spade lead, plays ace of diamonds and successfully finesses the jack. But now East has only to hold up the king of hearts for one round and South will still have problems. It must be assumed, too, that East will also be capable of holding up the king of hearts if he has K x only.

Thus the conclusion is that South should play for the drop in diamonds because the finesse, even if successful, will not necessarily win the contract.

Dealer, North   Neither side vulnerable

♠ A Q J 5
♡ A 7 4
◇ Q J 3
♣ A K 10

♠ 10 led

♠ 4
♡ Q 9 8 5 3
◇ A K 5
♣ Q J 6 2

South	West	North	East
—	—	2NT	pass
3♡	pass	4♡(1)	pass
6♡(2)	pass	pass	pass

Final contract—Six Hearts

(1) As his 2NT opening is not better than average in support of hearts, North should simply bid game and not make any other kind of forward move.

(2) North can hardly hold all the right cards for a grand slam, so the sensible course is to bid six, giving no further information to the opponents.

The early play

West leads the 10 of spades and declarer goes up with the ace. When the ace of hearts is led from dummy, East drops the king. How should South continue?

First look

If East's king of hearts is a true card, South can make the contract only by means of a trump end-play against West, who is apparently marked with J 10 x x of hearts.

Problem No. 57

South must aim to reduce West to J 10 x of hearts after ten tricks. Also he must hope that West will follow to three rounds of clubs. Otherwise, West will ruff the third club and still make another trump trick. This is the key to the correct order of play.

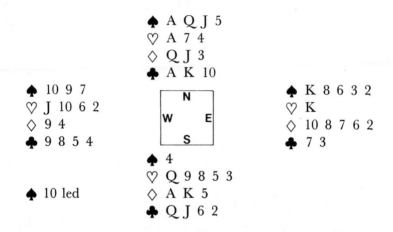

♠ 10 9 7
♥ J 10 6 2
♦ 9 4
♣ 9 8 5 4

♠ 10 led

Playing in six hearts, South wins the spade lead and lays down the ace of hearts, on which the king falls.

To execute an end-play against West's presumed J 10 x of hearts, South must extract all the cards that West holds in the side suits. Since the contract will never be made if West is short in clubs, South should play clubs early on. Finding that West holds four clubs, he plays off four rounds, discarding a diamond from dummy and ruffing a spade meanwhile. It will probably be possible to judge from the discards that West holds three spades and two diamonds rather than the other way round. South crosses to the queen of diamonds, therefore, ruffs another spade, cashes ace of diamonds and leads the 5 at trick eleven. West ruffs with the 10 of hearts and the last two tricks are won by South's Q 9.

If it turns out that East began with K x of hearts and has caused South to adopt a line of play that loses a lay-down contract, choose different opponents next time!

8. Opponents Make Mistakes, Too

Some of the problems towards the end of this section would not be easy to solve even with a sight of all the cards, and it would take a very quick-witted player to find the best play at the table. However, such situations are worth studying because they occur fairly often and are not so difficult once the basic idea is familiar. It is probably in this area—deceptions that cause a defender to miscount—that most advances will be made in the future.

Most of the routine deceptions in a single suit are well known. Here are a few that may not be so familiar:

1. Plays to conceal strength

Quite often, the first suit led against a notrump contract will not be the one that the declarer most fears. It may be essential to dissuade the opposition from switching to another suit when they take their first defensive trick.

7 5

4 led

A K J

There are two possibilities with this combination. The more obvious one is to win East's 10 with the king. But suppose East plays the queen: then it may be clever to play the jack and win the next trick with the ace. This will surely deceive East, if not West. The same play can be made with K x on the table, A J x in hand.

Sometimes the defenders will lead a five-card suit which you have concealed in the bidding.

9 2

4 led

A K J 7 3

When East plays the queen, don't win with the ace as though Christmas had come early. Play the 7 and gain a tempo. It is important to play the 7 because East, not having seen the 3, will think that his partner has a five-card suit.

This play has numerous variations. So, indeed, has the next:

7 5 4

K J 8 3 2   9 6

A Q 10

When West leads the 3 and East plays the 9, win with the queen. If West wins the first defensive trick he may follow with a low card of this suit; if East has the first entry, the play of the queen will have made no difference.

2. Plays to conceal weakness

Sometimes the play of a high card will give the appearance of an unblock from strength.

J 5 3

Q 10 8 4 2   A 9 6

K 7

When West leads the 4 and East plays the ace, drop the king. East may place you with K Q and look for a more dynamic attack.

J 4

K Q 8 5 2   A 7 6

10 9 3

In the middle of the play East leads the 6. Play the 9 and, when West plays the queen, gravely 'unblock' the jack. The same play can be made when dummy holds Q x.

Here your objective is to avoid losing two immediate tricks:

10 7 5 4

3   A Q J 9 8 6

K 2

West leads the 3 of a suit that his partner has bid. It may help to drop the king under the ace. East can safely continue the suit but he may look for a different attack. When dummy holds the jack this type of play obviously has a greater chance of success. Here the long suit is held by the opening leader:

J 8 5

A Q 10 9 7 6 2   4

K 3

West, who has shown seven-card length, leads the ace. By dropping the king, South may deter West from continuing the suit and it may be possible later to dispose of the second loser.

Dealer, South   Neither side vulnerable

♠ Q J
♡ K 7 2
◇ 10 7 4 3
♣ A J 6 4

♡ Q led

♠ 8 5 4 2
♡ A 8 5
◇ A K 6
♣ K Q 2

South	West	North	East
1♣	pass	1◇	pass
1NT(1)	pass	3NT	pass
pass	pass		

Final contract—3NT

(1) South follows this sequence to indicate a balanced hand of about 15–16 points, too strong for a weak notrump opening.

The early play

West leads the queen of hearts and East drops the 6. How should South plan the play?

First look

South has eight tricks on top and the diamonds offer reasonable prospects of a ninth. Meanwhile, there is a danger that when opponents win the lead they may take four tricks in spades.

Problem No. 58

There are various ways of looking for the ninth trick. Declarer might begin by winning the first trick and playing off four rounds of clubs. Opponents may make a wrong discard. On the other hand, if you show that you hold four tricks in clubs, the defenders will judge more easily that they must hope to make four tricks in spades when they gain the lead.

Technically, the best way to establish an extra trick in diamonds is to play off ace, king and another. This gains when East has a doubleton Q x or J x.

But when you fear a switch, as you do here, the best psychological plan is to let opponents obtain the lead before they have had much chance to assess what is going on.

```
                    ♠ Q J
                    ♡ K 7 2
                    ◇ 10 7 4 3
                    ♣ A J 6 4
  ♠ K 9 7 3       ┌─────────┐        ♠ A 10 6
  ♡ Q J 10 4      │    N    │        ♡ 9 6 3
  ◇ Q 8 2         │ W     E │        ◇ J 9 5
  ♣ 10 3          │    S    │        ♣ 9 8 7 5
                  └─────────┘
  ♡ Q led           ♠ 8 5 4 2
                    ♡ A 8 5
                    ◇ A K 6
                    ♣ K Q 2
```

South is in 3NT and West leads the queen of hearts. Suppose that declarer wins and plays off ace, king and another diamond. If West knows his onions he will switch to the king of spades, East will unblock the 10, and the defenders will take four spade tricks.

Tactically, it is better to win the first heart and lead a *low* diamond. Not so easy, then, for either defender to make the right switch. (If East is in, he must lead the 10 of spades.) The defenders will probably continue hearts and then, with the diamonds breaking 3–3, South will run nine tricks.

Dealer, South   Neither side vulnerable

$\spadesuit$ K 8 7 5 4 2
$\heartsuit$ 8 2
$\diamondsuit$ J 10
$\clubsuit$ 7 5 3

$\clubsuit$ Q led

$\spadesuit$ A 6
$\heartsuit$ A K Q J 9 5
$\diamondsuit$ A 7
$\clubsuit$ A K 4

South	West	North	East
2$\clubsuit$	pass	2$\diamondsuit$	pass
2$\heartsuit$	pass	2$\spadesuit$	pass
3$\heartsuit$	pass	4$\heartsuit$	pass
4NT(1)	pass	5$\clubsuit$	pass
5$\diamondsuit$	pass	6$\heartsuit$(2)	pass
pass	pass		

Final contract—Six Hearts

(1) South knows, of course, that North, holding no ace, will respond five clubs. He intends to follow with a try of five diamonds, meaning "If you have anything, I want to be in six."

(2) So far North has merely responded to forcing bids. He is entitled to think that his modest values will be worth at least one trick.

The early play

West leads the queen of clubs and East follows with the 2. How should South plan the play?

First look

Unfortunately, both hands have a doubleton in the same suit, and South may regret that he did not pass four hearts. There seems no obvious way of avoiding the loss of a diamond and a club.

Problem No. 59

There are faint squeeze possibilities. For example, South might win the club lead, draw trumps, and duck a diamond to improve the timing. Then if he can find the same opponent with three spades and five clubs there will be a squeeze in the black suits.

For this purpose, East's 2 of clubs at the first trick is not encouraging—it suggests that the clubs are divided 4–3. There is little chance of opponents making the wrong discards, because declarer's failure to play for a diamond ruff will mark him with a doubleton in this suit.

Against most defenders there is a better practical chance: try to lure them into an unwise overruff. Suppose that the cards lie like this:

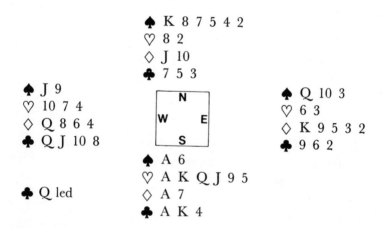

```
                 ♠ K 8 7 5 4 2
                 ♡ 8 2
                 ◊ J 10
                 ♣ 7 5 3
  ♠ J 9                          ♠ Q 10 3
  ♡ 10 7 4          N            ♡ 6 3
  ◊ Q 8 6 4       W   E          ◊ K 9 5 3 2
  ♣ Q J 10 8        S            ♣ 9 6 2
                 ♠ A 6
  ♣ Q led        ♡ A K Q J 9 5
                 ◊ A 7
                 ♣ A K 4
```

Playing in six hearts, South wins the club lead, plays ace and king of spades, then a third round, which he ruffs with the 9 of hearts. Now, if West overruffs, declarer can draw trumps, finishing in dummy, and discard his two losers on the established spades.

It is true that the overruff by West would be poor play—but have you not seen many worse things at the bridge table?

Dealer, South   E–W vulnerable

```
              ♠ K 10
              ♡ K 8 6 2
              ◇ J 10 8 7 5
              ♣ 6 3
  ♣ 5 led
              ♠ Q 9 3
              ♡ A Q 4
              ◇ A Q 6 2
              ♣ K J 9
```

South	West	North	East
1 ◇ (1)	pass	2 ◇ (2)	pass
2NT	pass	3NT	pass
pass	pass		

Final contract—3NT

(1) Outside the range for 1NT in South's system.

(2) For many players it is a criminal offence not to respond in a four-card major. On the other side there are these considerations: with a strong hand including four hearts, South can bid hearts himself on the next round; by responding two diamonds you prevent East from bidding spades at the level of one; and when you raise to two diamonds you have something in hand, whereas if you respond one heart and the bidding becomes competitive, it may be unsound to follow with support for diamonds at a high level.

The early play

West leads the 5 of clubs and East plays the 10. How should South plan the play?

First look

If South can pick up the king of diamonds he will make at least nine tricks. If not, he is in danger of losing a diamond, a spade and probably four clubs.

Problem No. 60

All players are familiar with the deceptive play of winning with the ace when they hold A Q x. To win with the king when you hold K J 9 is on occasions equally effective and more difficult for the defence to read.

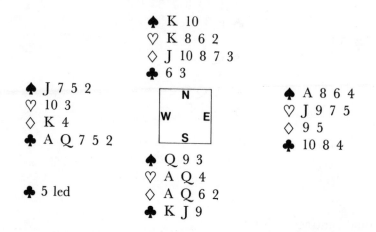

♠ K 10
♡ K 8 6 2
♢ J 10 8 7 3
♣ 6 3

♠ J 7 5 2
♡ 10 3
♢ K 4
♣ A Q 7 5 2

♠ A 8 6 4
♡ J 9 7 5
♢ 9 5
♣ 10 8 4

♣ 5 led

♠ Q 9 3
♡ A Q 4
♢ A Q 6 2
♣ K J 9

South is in 3NT, West leads the 5 of clubs and East plays the 10. Since he is liable to lose a diamond trick to West, not to East, South should take the first trick with the king of clubs, not the jack. Then he crosses to the king of hearts and runs the jack of diamonds, losing to the king.

From the play to the first trick West is likely to assume that his partner holds the jack of clubs. He may, therefore, under-lead the A Q, because to lay down the ace would be costly if East held J 10 alone.

There is no certainty about this, it is true, but what is quite certain is that if South won the first trick with the jack of clubs, West, when he came in with the king of diamonds, would switch to spades, hoping to find his partner with the ace.

Dealer, South   Both sides vulnerable

```
                    ♠ 8 5 3
                    ♡ K 8 4
                    ◇ K J 3
                    ♣ A K 10 9
♠ K led
                    ♠ A 9 6
                    ♡ A Q J 9 7 5 3 2
                    ◇ —
                    ♣ J 4
```

South	West	North	East
4♣(1)	pass	4◇(2)	pass
4♠	pass	5♣	pass
6♡(3)	pass	pass	pass

Final contract—Six Hearts

(1) South is playing a version of the Texas convention in which opening bids of four clubs and four diamonds indicate respectively a "strong" four heart or four spade opening.

(2) North's bid of the "intermediate" suit indicates simply that he sees a prospect of slam.

(3) South has heard enough; there is no reason to advertise the void in diamonds.

The early play

West leads the king of spades. It is unlikely that there could be any advantage in holding off, so South wins and leads the queen of hearts, West playing the 6. How should South continue?

First look

After the spade lead South cannot afford to give up a club. A direct finesse in clubs would produce thirteen tricks or ten tricks. Perhaps there is a more subtle approach?

Problem No. 61

There is more to the play than might be supposed. The declarer's first move should be to test his opponent's nerve.

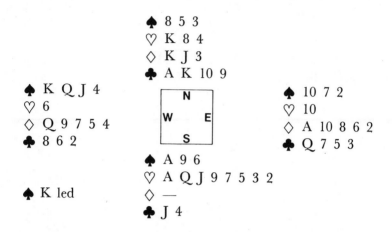

```
               ♠ 8 5 3
               ♡ K 8 4
               ◇ K J 3
               ♣ A K 10 9
♠ K Q J 4                        ♠ 10 7 2
♡ 6            ┌─────────┐       ♡ 10
◇ Q 9 7 5 4   │ N       │       ◇ A 10 8 6 2
♣ 8 6 2       │ W     E │       ♣ Q 7 5 3
              │    S    │
              └─────────┘
♠ K led        ♠ A 9 6
               ♡ A Q J 9 7 5 3 2
               ◇ —
               ♣ J 4
```

Playing in six hearts, South wins the spade lead and lays down the queen of hearts. Although the 10 does not appear from West, South overtakes with the king and leads the jack of diamonds from dummy. This is the card he would choose if he held a singleton queen, so East is under some pressure. He should, in fact, play low, because he can see that South must have losers in the black suits and can hardly have a loser in diamonds as well.

After he has ruffed the jack of diamonds South must consider whether to take a straightforward finesse in clubs or a ruffing finesse. The ruffing finesse is the better plan, not so much because it ensures one down at worst, as because it contains the additional chance, as compared with the direct finesse, of dropping a doubleton queen in the East hand. As the cards lie, the ruffing finesse brings in the twelfth trick.

One further point about the early play: it would not be good play to lead queen of hearts, then a heart to the king, as this would give West a chance to discard his lowest diamond, signifying an odd number and so making it easier for East to withhold the ace of diamonds.

Dealer, North   Both sides vulnerable

```
                     ♠ J 10
                     ♡ K 7 4 2
                     ◇ A 10 5 2
                     ♣ K J 8
   ♠ 5 led
                     ♠ A Q 9
                     ♡ A Q
                     ◇ K 6 3
                     ♣ 10 9 6 5 2
```

South	West	North	East
—	—	1 ◇	pass
3NT(1)	pass	pass	pass

Final contract—3NT

(1) It is seldom a good idea to respond 3NT on anything other than 4–3–3–3 distribution, but here there does not seem to be any good alternative. South has tenaces in both major suits and the clubs are not worth mentioning.

The early play

West leads the 5 of spades, the jack is played from dummy, and East follows with the 3. (Opponents lead fourth best in principle.) How should South plan the play?

First look

To arrive at nine tricks, South will need to develop the clubs. The obvious danger is that the opponents will establish tricks in spades before the ace and queen of clubs have been forced out.

Problem No. 62

If South plays this hand in straightforward fashion, over-taking the jack of spades with the queen and running the 10 of clubs, he will lose the contract when East has Q x or Q x x of clubs and West has five or six spades to the king.

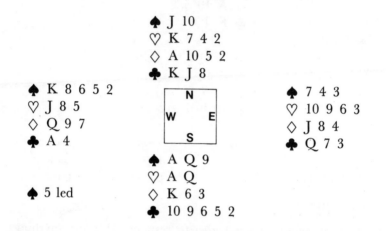

♠ J 10
♡ K 7 4 2
◇ A 10 5 2
♣ K J 8

♠ K 8 6 5 2   ♠ 7 4 3
♡ J 8 5   ♡ 10 9 6 3
◇ Q 9 7   ◇ J 8 4
♣ A 4   ♣ Q 7 3

♠ 5 led

♠ A Q 9
♡ A Q
◇ K 6 3
♣ 10 9 6 5 2

South is in 3NT and West leads the 5 of spades. The danger is that East will win the first club and return a spade, enabling West to clear the suit. To lessen the risk, South should win the spade lead in dummy and lead the 4 of clubs from the table. It is quite difficult for East to go up with the queen from Q x or Q x x. If East fails to play the queen, the contract will be safe.

Since South is secure against a further spade lead from West, the lead of the low club from dummy cannot cost, however the suit is distributed. If West holds Q x, for example, and wins the first club, he can do no damage. Opportunities for this kind of backward finesse are frequent.

Dealer, South   Neither side vulnerable

<pre>
                    ♠ A 5
                    ♡ K 6 4 2
                    ◇ J 8 4
                    ♣ A J 5 3
        ♣ 8 led
                    ♠ K J 10 9 8 4
                    ♡ A J 10 9 8
                    ◇ —
                    ♣ Q 6
</pre>

South	West	North	East
1♠	pass	2♣	pass
2♡	pass	4♡	pass
6♡(1)	pass	pass	pass

Final contract—Six Hearts

(1) North might hold the wrong cards, so technically it would be sounder to indicate the diamond control and leave the next move to partner. However, South has decided to gamble and does not wish to give a picture of his hand.

The early play

West leads the 8 of clubs. How should South plan the play?

First look

Players sometimes underlead a king through dummy's suit, but South cannot be too sanguine about the clubs. He must decide how to play to the first trick and how to manage the trumps.

Problem No. 63

To take a losing finesse in clubs at trick one would not necessarily be fatal, but South would then need to pick up the queen of hearts. There are, however, chances to make the contract even if the club king is on the wrong side and South misguesses the hearts.

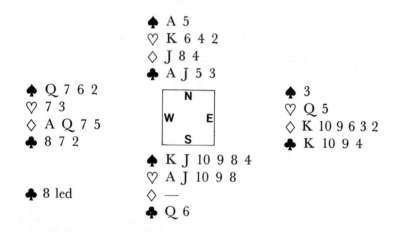

```
                    ♠ A 5
                    ♡ K 6 4 2
                    ◇ J 8 4
                    ♣ A J 5 3
 ♠ Q 7 6 2          ┌──────────┐          ♠ 3
 ♡ 7 3              │    N     │          ♡ Q 5
 ◇ A Q 7 5          │ W      E │          ◇ K 10 9 6 3 2
 ♣ 8 7 2            │    S     │          ♣ K 10 9 4
                    └──────────┘
                    ♠ K J 10 9 8 4
 ♣ 8 led            ♡ A J 10 9 8
                    ◇ —
                    ♣ Q 6
```

South plays in six spades and West, taking the view that declarer can always cope with a lead in the unbid suit, opens the 8 of clubs.

It is unlikely that the club finesse will be right and South should attempt a stratagem that will give him a chance even if he does not find the queen of hearts. He should go up with the ace of clubs, dropping the queen from hand. Then he crosses to the ace of hearts and runs the jack.

This line will give him an excellent chance, obviously, if West has Q x x in hearts. As the cards lie, the jack loses to East's queen. But will it be clear to East that he should lay down the king of clubs, perhaps allowing South to ruff and later discard a singleton diamond on the jack of clubs?

If East leads a diamond instead of the king of clubs, South will discover the spade position on the second round of the suit and be able to set up sufficient discards to dispose of dummy's clubs.

Dealer, South   Neither side vulnerable

♠ J 4
♡ K J 7 2
◇ Q 8 5 3
♣ A Q 9

♠ 9 led

♠ A
♡ 10 3
◇ A K J 10 9 7
♣ K J 6 2

South	West	North	East
1 ◇	pass	1 ♡	pass
3 ◇ (1)	pass	4 ♣ (2)	pass
5 ♣ (3)	pass	5 ◇	pass
6 ◇	pass	pass	pass

Final contract—Six Diamonds

(1) North-South were playing a one-club system, so South was maximum for his one diamond opening. A rebid of two clubs would have given a wrong picture.

(2) North proposes to go to five diamonds at least and makes an advance cue-bid on the way.

(3) South cannot be sure whether four clubs is a suit or a control, but either way it cannot be wrong to raise.

The early play

West leads the 9 of spades. In such situations it is generally good play to put in the high card from dummy, so declarer puts on the jack and wins the queen with the ace. All follow to a round of trumps. How should South continue?

First look

The contract will depend, evidently, on not losing more than one heart trick. If the ace and queen are divided South may have to guess. He must consider whether there is any way in which he can tilt the odds to his advantage. South is playing in a pairs event, where extra tricks are important to both sides.

Problem No. 64

With a doubleton opposite K J x x it is often good tactics to lead the suit early on, before the defenders have been able to get any count. That play certainly puts West under pressure when the cards lie in this fashion:

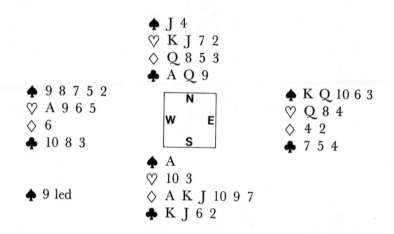

```
                    ♠ J 4
                    ♡ K J 7 2
                    ◇ Q 8 5 3
                    ♣ A Q 9
   ♠ 9 8 7 5 2                        ♠ K Q 10 6 3
   ♡ A 9 6 5          N               ♡ Q 8 4
   ◇ 6            W       E           ◇ 4 2
   ♣ 10 8 3           S               ♣ 7 5 4
                    ♠ A
   ♠ 9 led         ♡ 10 3
                    ◇ A K J 10 9 7
                    ♣ K J 6 2
```

Playing in six diamonds, South puts in the jack of spades from dummy and wins the queen with the ace. One of the reasons for playing the jack is that East is obliged to cover and so cannot give any clue to his length in the suit. Now, if a heart is led after one round of trumps, West has an awkward decision, for if South held a doubleton spade and a singleton heart it would be fatal to duck. Moreover, West must make up his mind quickly: it is no use hesitating, then playing low.

Thus, to lead a heart at trick two is a fair answer, but South can make a subtle play that will improve his chances still further. He draws a second trump, then plays four rounds of clubs, discarding a *spade* from the table. West, playing in a pairs event, will be noting South's distribution and may well conclude, from the spade discard, that South's shape is 2–1–6–4. Then, to save the overtrick, he will go up with the ace of hearts on the first round, resolving the guess.

Dealer, West   Neither side vulnerable

♠ J 9 7 3
♡ K 8 5
◇ 7 2
♣ K 9 6 3

◇ 10 led

♠ A Q 10 8 2
♡ 10 4
◇ K 5 3
♣ A 8 5

South	West	North	East
—	1 ♡	pass	2 ◇
2 ♠	pass	4 ♠(1)	pass
pass	pass		

Final contract—Four Spades

(1) North is perhaps not worth more than three-and-a-half spades, but in such circumstances it is good for partnership morale to make the slight overbid rather than leave partner to make another borderline decision.

The early play

West leads the 10 of diamonds. East wins with the ace and returns the 7 of hearts. West wins with the ace and leads back the queen of hearts to dummy's king, East following suit. How should South plan the play?

First look

South has lost two tricks and the king of spades is almost sure to be wrong. Declarer must form some plan that may help him to avoid the loss of a club as well.

Problem No. 65

This is a difficult problem, because the declarer is likely to think that the solution lies in organizing a ruff-and-discard elimination. His first idea will be to cash the ace of spades, ruff the third round of each red suit, cash the ace and king of clubs, then exit with a spade. If West began with K x of spades and only two clubs he will be forced to concede a trick with his next lead.

The flaw in this plan is that West can hardly have the 2–6–3–2 distribution which the elimination play would require. If West had that distribution, East would hold only a moderate hand with five diamonds and would have responded 1NT, not two diamonds. This is a much more likely division:

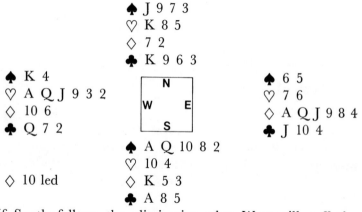

```
                    ♠ J 9 7 3
                    ♡ K 8 5
                    ◇ 7 2
                    ♣ K 9 6 3
  ♠ K 4                 ┌─────┐          ♠ 6 5
  ♡ A Q J 9 3 2         │  N  │          ♡ 7 6
  ◇ 10 6              W │     │ E         ◇ A Q J 9 8 4
  ♣ Q 7 2               │  S  │          ♣ J 10 4
                       └─────┘
                    ♠ A Q 10 8 2
                    ♡ 10 4
  ◇ 10 led          ◇ K 5 3
                    ♣ A 8 5
```

If South follows the elimination plan West will ruff the third round of diamonds with the king of spades and lead a club.

The contract may seem impossible as the cards lie, but South can make a good try. After the defenders have taken the two red aces and exited with a heart, South ruffs a heart, cashes the king of diamonds and the ace of spades, then leads a second spade. Now West, if he is the counting type, may think that as South has not attempted to ruff a third diamond his distribution must be 5–2–2–4. In which case, West may conclude, there is no reason to risk a lead from the queen of clubs: just lead a heart and concede a "useless" ruff-and-discard . . .